Diatribal Writes *of* Passage *in a* World *of* Wintertextuality

Poems on Language, Media, and Life (but not as we know it)

Language in Action Series

Lance Strate

Institute of General Semantics

Published by the Institute of General Semantics
72-11 Austin Street, #233
Forest Hills, New York, 11375
www.generalsemantics.org

Cover & Interior Book Design by Scribe Freelance
www.scribefreelance.com

ISBN: 978-1-970164-02-2 (Paperback)
978-1-970164-03-9 (eBook)

Printed in the United States of America

LIBRARY OF CONGRESS CATALOGING-IN-PUBLICATION DATA

Names: Strate, Lance, author.
Title: Diatribal writes of passage in a world of wintertextuality : poems
   on language, media, and life (but not as we know it) / Lance Strate.
Description: Forest Hills : Institute of General Semantics, 2020. | Series:
Language in action series | Summary: "The second poetry collection by Lance
Strate, this volume brings together an eclectic mix of poems that address the
themes of language, communication, media, technology, and poetry itself, etc"--
Provided by publisher.
Identifiers: LCCN 2020001266 (print) | LCCN 2020001267 (ebook) | ISBN
9781970164022 (trade paperback) | ISBN 9781970164039 (kindle edition)
Subjects: LCGFT: Poetry.
Classification: LCC PS3569.T6913275 D53 2020 (print) | LCC
PS3569.T6913275
   (ebook) | DDC 813/.6--dc23
LC record available at https://lccn.loc.gov/2020001266
LC ebook record available at https://lccn.loc.gov/2020001267

The **Language in Action** series, sponsored by the Institute of General Semantics, publishes books devoted to creative modes of expression that can open the doors of perception, and foster better understandings of the nature of language, symbols, communication, and the semantic, technological, and media environments that we inhabit. Through processes of play and probing, art can bring into awareness alternative forms of experience and evaluation to the everyday, routine, taken-for-granted world. It can also shed new light on mind and method, consciousness and culture, abstracting and attention, ecology and enlightenment, and, most important to students of general semantics, science and sanity.

Founded in 1938 by Alfred Korzybski, the Institute of General Semantics promotes, in the words of S.I. Hayakawa, *the study of how not be a damn fool.* As a non-aristotelian system devoted to enhancing human potential, general semantics has inspired numerous novelists, poets, artists, musicians, and creative thinkers. General semantics today is devoted to explorations of meaning and the meaning of meaning, of metaphors and memes, archetypes and arts, symbols and signals, signs and significance, codes and ciphers, sense perception and sense-making, and the vast variety of ways of seeing, feeling, and thinking that humanity is heir to. The quarterly journal of the IGS, *ETC: A Review of General Semantics*, has been publishing essays, research, and literary work since 1943.

About the Author

LANCE STRATE HAS BEEN LABELED as an educator, public speaker, writer, and poet, as well as some other, less benign designations. His poetry has been published in *ETC: A Review of General Semantics*, *KronoScope*, *Explorations in Media Ecology*, *Anekaant*, the *General Semantics Bulletin*, and *Poetica Magazine*, as well as several anthologies. His first poetry collection, *Thunder at Darwin Station*, was published by NeoPoesis Press in 2015, as was the anthology of creative work he co-edited with Adeena Karasick, *The Medium is the Muse: Channeling Marshall McLuhan*. His other books include *Echoes and Reflections* (2006), *On the Binding Biases of Time* (2011), *Amazing Ourselves to Death* (2014), and *Media Ecology* (2017). He also has a number of other co-edited volumes to his credit, among them *Communication and Cyberspace* (1996, 2003), *The Legacy of McLuhan* (2005), *Korzybski And...* (2012), and *Taking Up McLuhan's Cause* (2017).

Dr. Strate earned his PhD with Neil Postman at New York University, and holds the title of Professor of Communication and Media Studies at Fordham University in New York City, as well as serving as a Trustee and former Executive Director of the Institute of General Semantics, President of the New York Society for General Semantics, a founder and board member of the Media Ecology Association, and a past President of the New York State Communication Association.

Lance Strate received the New York State Communication Association's 2019 Neil Postman Mentor Award and their 1998 John F. Wilson Fellow Award (in recognition for exceptional scholarship, leadership, and dedication to the field of communication), the Eastern Communication Association's 2019 Distinguished Research Fellow Award, the Media Ecology Association's 2018 Marshall McLuhan Award for Outstanding Book (for *Media Ecology: An Approach to Understanding the Human Condition*) and their 2013 Walter J. Ong Award for Career Achievement in Scholarship. He delivered the 2018 Alfred Korzybski Memorial Lecture, and Denver

Mayor Wellington E. Webb proclaimed "that February 15, 2002 be known as Dr. Lance Strate Day in the City and County of Denver" in honor of the keynote address he gave for the Rocky Mountain Communication Association.

Lance has written comedy and humor, op-eds, lay sermons and prayers, an episode of the nationally syndicated children's animated television program *Adventures of the Galaxy Rangers*, several multimedia presentations, many blog posts, and close to 200 essays. Translations of his writing have appeared in French, Spanish, Italian, Portuguese, Hungarian, Hebrew, Mandarin, and Quenya.

Acknowledgements

THE COVER IMAGE, "Vincent van Gogh Invents the Satellite Weather Map," was created by Edward Wachtel, and used here with his kind permission. It was the inspiration for the poem, "Hurricane Vinny."

In slightly modified form, the following poems were previously published:

- "a fickle pickle," "a turn of the phrase," "an account, Korzybski old chap, of this thing of ours," "Ana, log out," "the art of facts," "cross I'd twisted tongue," "flushing," and "my system" in *ETC: A Review of General Semantics*;
- "beggared," "unsaid words," "questions," "genesis," "air," and "the poet" first appeared in *Anekaant: A Journal of Polysemic Thought*;
- "getting an ear fuel" was published online by the *Malahat Review* as winner of the Twitter Monostich Poetry Contest, August 27, 2012;
- "word high" and "these words" appeared in the *General Semantics Bulletin*;
- "hurricane Vinny" and "in the age of show business" were published in *Explorations in Media Ecology*;
- "blog versus," "a brief history of the blogverse," and "the hunters' love," were included in an anthology entitled *Online Poetry* in conjunction with being listed as a finalist for 2008 Poet of the Year by Poetry Blog Rankings;
- "chirography" was published in the collection called *Candy*, edited by Dale Winslow and Erin Badough, published by NeoPoiesis Press;
- "prose" and "the medium is…" were among my contributions to *The Medium is the Muse: Channeling Marshall McLuhan*, which I co-edited with Adeena Karasick, also published by NeoPoiesis Press.

I am grateful to Corey Anton, Chair of the Publishing Committee of the Institute of General Semantics, and to Martin Levinson, IGS President, for making this publication possible, and to Daniel Middleton for his efforts in getting this volume ready for publication.

A very special thank you goes to Dale Winslow of NeoPoesis Press for her longstanding support and for showing me the way forward along poetic pathways. I would also like to thank my other friends at NeoPoesis, Stephen Roxborough and Erin Badough.

Most of the poems in this volume were first put out into the world on my blog on the old MySpace social network, now gone as if it had never been. The name I gave to my blog was BlogVersed, and this collection includes the poems that explicitly refer to the blog in self-reflexive fashion. I make no claims as to their artistic merit, at the very start I referred to my efforts as Vogon poetry, and the poems remain the verbal equivalent of a hyperspace bypass. Poetry does allow for an alternate means of expressing ideas, and much of the work collected here is based on my study of communication, media ecology, and of course general semantics; the intent has been to provoke thought, share my understandings, perhaps also to entertain. And I owe the online poetry community that once populated MySpace much for the inspiration, feedback, and motivation that they gave me. While it is impossible to name everyone that I encountered there, Si Philbrook especially stands out, and this volume includes a poem I wrote for his birthday. Another great inspiration was Robert Priest, an accomplished and prolific poet and songwriter. Again, Dale Winslow was an important part of that community as well.

Other friends who contributed in one way or another to my creative output include Ed Wachtel, Paul Levinson, Eric McLuhan, Valerie Peterson, Gerald Erion, Marty Friedman, Heather Crandall, Elena Lamberti, Camille Paglia, Samantha Markus, Ted Baker, Devkumar Trivedi, and Balvant Parekh.

I am indebted to Bini BS and Ed Tywoniak for their encouragement and editorial support. And my gratitude also extends to TC McLuhan, Teresa Manzella, Mike Plugh, Thom Gencarelli, Paolo Granata, Adeena Karasick, bill bissett, BW Powe, Bob Blechman, Nora Bateson, Jackie Rudig, Bob Albrecht, Elena Lamberti, Barry Schwartz, and so many others.

I am much obliged to Fordham University, and especially to my colleagues and students, as well as to my colleagues in the Media Ecology Association, and of course, the Institute of General

Semantics. Thank you too to everyone associated with the Poetry Garden group at Congregation Adas Emuno of Leonia, New Jersey.

Finally, I am every grateful for the foundation provided by my family, beginning with my mother, Betty Strate, and my father Benjamin Strate, both of blessed memory, and extending to my wife, Barbara, my son Benjamin, and my daughter, Sarah.

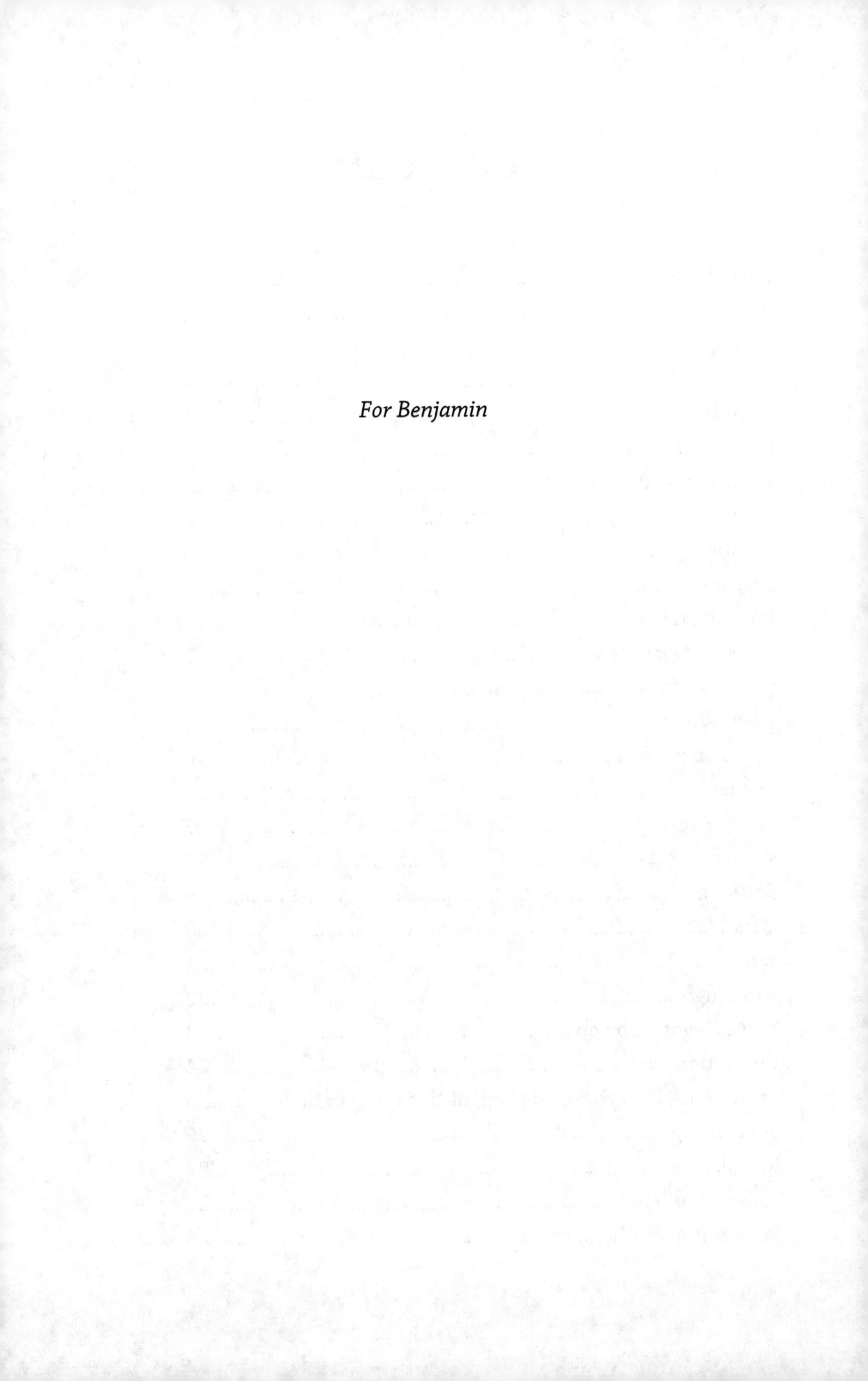

For Benjamin

Contents

up in smoke

these pages caught fire
these words were consumed
only ashes were left of them
they disappeared for all time
no one will ever read
what was written here
that's the way it goes sometimes
we struggle in vain

mystery

I recall when I was very young
my parents took me to the movies
with them

and I saw those giant faces
on the screen
and I saw their lips move

and I heard the words they spoke
familiar sounds

I could almost sense their meaning
almost
almost
almost

but no

I couldn't
understand
what
they were
saying

adult talk was a foreign language to me

   I dozed off

over half a century later
it's still a mystery
to me

syntagm

a detail of the moment
a seemingly trivial object
connected to a natural or architectural setting
intensifying vision, hearing
smell, taste   or touch
leading to a fading but still vivid recollection
a memory of a man, woman, or child
someone of some significance
once present   now absent
returning in the form of thought
conversation
observation
motivating a metaphor
putting in motion new meanings
framing the elements so that the parts hang together in a novel
     arrangement
introducing a theory or hypothesis
about the nature of our collective existence
reality
biology
spirituality
leading to an emotion
deeply felt   profoundly expressed
coupled with a peculiar and unforgettable sense perception
linked to the time remembered
linked to the lingering aftereffects, the residue that remains
linked to the experience of the now
linked to the act of composition
linked to the wry conclusion
let x=y
let y=z
let it go!

you

I wrote this poem for *you*
for *you*, and only for *you*
others may read it
but it was not written for their eyes
others may mouth the words
but they were meant for *your* lips alone
others may be listening in
as I whisper these lines into *your* ears
but I am saying them only to *you*
others may think that they are the one
that I am speaking to
let them think what they will
they are not the one
it is *you*, and only *you*
and *you* may question
whether it is really *you*
and not someone else
but know, and know well and sure
it is *you*
you are the one
you are the only one
you
and *you* may wonder how it is
that I have singled *you* out
why *you* are the chosen one
when all along *you* thought *you* were
just a lonely face in the crowd
safe and comfortable in *your* anonymity
hiding in the plain sight
of *your* page or screen?
but deep down, *you* know
you know *you* are the one
you know why *you* are the one
why *you* are special
you know
and *you* know that if *you* were to ask me
am *I* the one?
is it really *me*?
I would not be able to answer *you*

it's just not possible
under the circumstances
maybe someday...
but for the time being
you will just have to trust me
and accept that it is *you*
and that only *you*
and I
know the truth
that we cannot speak of it
that it shall remain our silent secret
that it is *you*
you are the one
you are the only one
you

the poet

The poet sneezes
calls it poetry
the dog has fleas
and scratches
calls it naught
calls it not
calls its knot
hanky please

flushing

early November
first snow
that eerie lake effect
buckshot fired from the jet stream
wet and messy and cold
welcome to buffalo

my host, the philosopher
speaks of the ethics of plumbing
the morality of pipes
the consciousness of toilets and sinks
and the mediation of stalls

I speak to the first semester students
about images and immediacy
about critical thinking
and crap detectors
the words pour out of my mouth
wet and messy and cold
and the students, they go
flush

the
meaning
of
meaning

balanced on a ladder
afraid to climb
about to fall
I met an angel coming down
a better angel
than I had known before
I lifted my arms
to shield my head
as the angel pummeled me
I took the blows
could not fight back
prayed for an end to pain
prayed to become as stone
and drop to the earth again
and then
this
is what
the angel
tolled
to me:

you know,
the meaning of meaning is meaning
it's an inclination, a leaning
it's an angle, will you take the bait?
hurry now, or you might be late!

a turn of a phrase

a turn of a phrase
can go on for days
it's a merry-go-round
of meaning and sound

a turn of a phrase
is a spinning top
it can make you dizzy
'til it comes to a stop

a turn of a phrase
is a Hanukah dreidel
it won't stand for long
it's fundamentally unstable

a turn of a phrase
is a Whirling Dervish
dancing in a manner
more than a little curvish

a turn of a phrase
is a voyeur's gaze
when you're least aware
it makes you stop and stare

a turn of a phrase
is a crazy carousel
ride the painted ponies
and fall under its spell

a turn of a phrase
is a spinning wheel
if you prick your finger
it might never heal

a turn of a phrase
is a turn of the key
it can open your mind
and unlock mystery

a turn of a phrase
is an endless maze
just around the bend
is another dead end

a turn of a phrase
like a turn of the screw
tightens its grip
trapping me and you

a turn of a phrase
is a linguistic maelström
a whirlpool of words
you may never escape from

a turn of a phrase
is like the Earth on its axis
day follows night
like death follows taxes

a turn of a phrase
is a roundabout
whether you're coming or going
it's hard to get out

a turn of a phrase
is a revolving door
better exit quickly
or you'll be in for more

a turn of a phrase
is just a phase
of language gone mad
it's a passing fad

a turn of a phrase
is just circular reasoning
it's gourmet cooking
with spices and seasoning

a turn of a phrase
is a centrifugal force
with great gravity
a weighty discourse

a turn of a phrase
swings and sways
like a pendulum do
that's English for you

questions

there are questions without answers
but no answers without questions
and the answer to each question
is a question in disguise

beggared

I begged the question
I got down on my knees

    pleading

  Please

                                                                 Please

    Please
        Please
            Please

but the question was not kind

    No
    No

the question was cold

      having no mercy and no sympathy
    No
the question had no answers for me

I begged the question

                                                  If you please

  but the question
            begged
                 to differ

breaking news

I've been thinking lately about breaks

about coffee breaks
and bone breaks
and day breaks and

line breaks (or should I say break
lines and break
points?)

about the good breaks and the bad breaks and the clean breaks and
the dirty breaks and prison breaks and commercial breaks (and how
to break the ice, break a leg, break dance, and break wind)

about the break downs and the break ups and the break ins and the
break outs
(not to mention the breakaways)

about giving a break
and taking a break

about the oddity of breaks
and never giving a sucker an even one

oops, guess it's time for a

cross I'd twisted tongue

if the former were the latter
and the latter were the former
then the former would come later
and the latter would come first

if the latter were the former
and the former were the latter
and you put them on a ladder
then the former would be high
and the latter would be low

if the former were the latter
and the latter were the former
and you made each one a letter
then the latter would be A
that would be the latter's letter
while the former would be B
yes, that's B, as in better

if the latter were the former
and the former were the latter
would the latter leave you colder
while the former leaves you warmer

if the former were the latter
and the latter were the former
you'd reform the former former
to become the latter latter
likewise the former latter
would now be the latter former

if the latter were the former
and the former were the latter
and you had the latter former
and you had the former latter
and you had the latter latter
and you had the former former
would you say, what does it matter?
would you tell them all to scatter?
or would you put them in their place?
would that be your saving grace?

these words

these words, these words are not my own
I simply take them out on loan
I borrow them, just for a time
just long enough to make this rhyme
and then return them to their source
how could I keep them here by force?
it's in their nature to be free
these words have got the best of me...

these words have lived upon the earth
for years and years before my birth
these words will not just disappear
when I am called away from here
I live and die inside these sounds
I cannot venture outside their bounds
I'm locked inside their prison cell
I'm trapped and glamoured by their spell

these words surround me, keep me warm
they give me shelter from the storm
I float on them and sail their sea
they clothe me and they nourish me
I breathe them in, I breathe them out
I need them without any doubt
they mold and shape me to their ways
they rule my nights, and govern my days

my thoughts are words, they shape my mind
my world is words, I am defined
by words I do not own, you see
these words have got the best of me...

when Woman made Words

Woman made Words
and taught them to Man

and Man said
  what a funny game you play
  with your mouth
  what a funny little game

and Woman said
  now we need to talk
  now you need to listen
  and now you need to do as you are told

and Man said
  this funny little game
  is not for me
  take back your Words
  that you made
  I do not want them anymore
  I just want to do things
  and look at things
  and eat things
  and grunt and growl

and Woman said
  too late Man
  too late

egged on my face

Ovaries are over easy (but men know pause, too). It varies, says Aries. Depends upon the dairies (or so Mammy reasons). Oh, very good, oh, very good, whispers Arial, all that flesh is hairy too, and so to err is you, man! Ovals are serious, you must be delirious, cries Eris! Oh, verily, you hover easily eastwards in oscillating existence on this vernal equinox, says Sirius. Of eerie us I sing! We need an overview, warns Bird, come, enter our aeries, and do not despair. Oy vey, responds Mary, ovations come easy! Men know puzzling contradiction. Women live it.

fashion

vested interests aside
I wonder when three-piece suits
will be back in style?

up an octave

No.
I'm not.
Lying.
Nope.
No siree.
Not me.
I.
Didn't.
Do it.
Don't know.
Who did.
But.
It wasn't.
Me.
No.
Nope.
It's true.
I swear.
It's true.
Not me.
No lie.
No.

sitting

I speak and you speak
sometimes we take turns
sometimes you forget that
I'm even there
and just go on talking
you speak
then you sleep
it's okay
I'll listen
I know you just want to
get it all out while you can
get it all out again and again
you speak again
I've heard it all before
again and again
you speak
and I listen
we speak at the same time
and you can't hear what I said
you don't know that I'm talking too
you just speak
and that's okay now
that's okay
it's what you need to do now
it's just what you need to do

and/or

a slow win's better than a fast draw
lost in the glow of sunset
bright red flow of fading light
unveiling toil's last reward
here rows are planted in the ground
trenches gouged by grave riders
departing for the day's end
watered by wounds still fresh
soiled garments
torn flesh and
drops of life
dampening seeds sown of stone
smooth surfaces underground
markers made from wood and rock
remain to tell the tale
that once upon a time
gifts were shared
over brief sojourns
they came and they went
just passing through
but the words
the words are with us still
the stories still
we tell
the echoes endure
the echoes endure
the echoes endure

gifts

give me language that lingers
alone without languor

language that longs
as it licks at lost memory

language that's lanky
with legs that are lengthy

language that lunges
and maybe gets lucky

language that links
to locations little known

language that unlocks
the keys to alignment

language that lights up
the dark night with laughter

language with lungs
loud enough that they'll listen

in lands everlasting
in longitudes sublime

give me language to speak
when all else are silent

give me language to call
to call out your name

welcome

words make worlds
worlds make words
whirling all the while
wandering where they will
watch them wind away

worlds make words
words make worlds
whirling all the while
wandering where they will
watch them wind away

worlds are our womb
words are our way
welcome to the wild

words are our womb
worlds are our way
welcome to the one

word high

Some antics
make 'im grin, or grim, but would a
gram mar
'is thinkin'? Would the wages of
sin tax
'im so very utterly? Indeed
sin own 'im
rest his soul
Ant own 'im
and bug, and worm. Remember when 'e
ate a mole? Oh, gee!
And you sez
Dick, shun Aries!
Rambo's a bad sign!
And I sez, 'e can't 'ear us, 'e's
deaf. Finishin'
it all up, so get in that fancy
vogue cab. You leery?
Don't be!
Thus, soar us
ever higher
never mind you shootin' up that
morph—holy geez
man! Listen to the
phone, it ticks
it taps. Don't
dial, Alex
it's too risky, man! They'll have the
ax sent
over, and then... kaput!
That's just how the
English languish
today!

oops, forgot who you are...

names are a nuisance
too many to remember
you look like a Mary
what?
your name is Kim?

too many people have the same name
too confusing to recall
your name's Jessica, right?
no? Amy? no?

don't tell me
I know I knew
once upon a time
long ago
in one year and out the other
Monica, is that your moniker?
no?

can't we just do without?
what's the point of all this
false sense of intimacy
just to confirm
acknowledge
please
that loathsome ego?

don't we know who we are?
we don't need names
can't it be enough to say
hey you? hey there... you?
it's so good to see you... you?

wouldn't that make us all the same?
equality
one for all for one and all?
wouldn't that make us all
one?

my system

what's solid is a fluid
that's moving very slow. . . .
what's fluid is not substance
it's energy aflow~~~

some 14 billion years ago
there was this great big POP!
an explosion so tremendous it
may never, ever stop

we are riders on the Big Bang
of the universal birth
clinging to some debris that
we call the planet Earth—

it's all a matter of scale
and perspective, don't you see?
it's all a matter of where you stand
and relativity:

things are not as they seem. . . .
things are not as they appear. . . .
so please be careful, and be kind
and have another beer!

an account, Korzybski old chap,
of this thing of ours

a word is not a thing
it's a thing that is not a thing, or
it's not a thing like other things
a word is not a *thing-thing*

a thing can be many things
this thing or that thing
one thing or the other thing,
a thing or *the* thing
your own thing or my thing
anything but a *word-thing*

a thing therefore I am
a *thing-thing*, not a *word-thing* am I
a name is not a man or woman
a *name-thing* is not me

but a thing is not a thing, no neither
a *thing-thing* is still
a *word-thing*, I fear
I sing of things
of *thing-things* and *word-things*
a thing, therefore, iambic or free

thing is, things are not what they seem
things are what they are not, *not-things*
the thing of things reigns without a rule
over *not-things* and *name-things*
word-things, and *thing-things* too

a thing is nothing if not a *not-thing*
and words are sweet *knot-things*
to tangle us up
what we say of things
is not the way of things
but the secret of things is
th'-*i-n-g*-ing

some things

things gone missing
things not found
things just out of reach
things gotten out of hand
things gotten into your head
things best left unsaid
things best not known by mortal man
things bought and paid for
things served and rendered
things stashed away for a rainy day
things hiding under the bed
things to do
things undone
things decided upon
things up in the air
things buried out of sight
things talked to death
things from another world
things unknown
things unnamed
things unaccounted for
things uncollected
things recollected
things past
things nowadays
things to come
things all considered
things ill considered
things of no apparent value
things first first
things finer in life
things blessed
things damnedest
things that go bump in the night
things all bright and beautiful
things being what they are
things not what they seem
things turning out not as expected
things that cannot be explained

things going on
things going off
things to see
things to be

air

the map dilates the territory
the clock dilutes the tarry tarry
the word delights the thin git
   rap resents
the cymbal dials for thee

called to order

Waiter! Waiter!
I do not *want* to know your name
I o n l y *want*
not to
wait!

something or other

something's going
something's coming
something's going on
something's coming off
something's going in
something's coming out
something's going down
something's coming up
something's going round
something's coming through
something's going across
something's coming between
something's going before
something's coming about
something's going past
something's coming forward
something's going by
something's coming to

                                                                but

some things never change

a fickle pickle

Pluto, O Pluto, O what did you do to deserve
such a brutal fate?
some say, God damn it, you are a planet and
nine is a number divine
others say, can't sugar coat it, we just have to
demote it, here's where we draw the line

Pluto, dear Pluto, please say it ain't true to me
please say it isn't too late
some say your addition, has become our
tradition, you're a body that's heavenly sent
others say, we can't avoid, that you're an
asteroid, science has no room for sentiment

Pluto, my Pluto, the question is moot to you
as you make your icy, erratic rounds
the words that we choose, the terms that we
use, make no difference to you all the same
you are what you are, an object so far away
immune to the attractions of fame
ignoring our mockery, you're just a big rock
you see, but the children all know your name

But Pluto, our Pluto, O surely you do know
how our mortal foolishness abounds
exiling you from the planetarium, we belong
in a sanitarium, for being so terribly inconstant
we are so very mad, that I think our next fad
will make Australia an island, not a continent

the art of facts

facts are facts
and that is that
when it comes to facts

facts are factual
and that is all you need to know
that facts are actual
except when they are not

actually, facts are satisfactory
except when they are not

facts are de facto actual
and it is factual to say
that facts are artifacts
and artifacts are artificial

as a matter of fact
facts are manufactured
facts are manufactured in a factory
factor that in, if you please:
facts are reasonable facsimiles
manufactured rather matter-of-factually
artifacts manufactured artificially

go tell your factotum
it won't matter
and that's a fact

and factor in that new factory odor
because facts are olfactory
and facts can be putrefactive
when artifacts are no longer active

now, don't strain your faculties
but there are facts that are true
and facts that are false
and facts somewhere in-between

you see, facts have many facets
there are facts that benefit benefactors
and facts that abet malefactors

mainly, facts may be multifaceted
indeed, they may be manufactured to be
that's the artifice of facsimile

facts are fickle
facts are feckless
facts are fractured
yes, it's a fact
and that is that

now, focus on the factors
that make up the facts
de facto factors that fact you all up
just the facts, ma'am, just the facts
just the facts
all the facts
and nothing but

focus on the facts now
focus all up
focus all up
focus all up
facts will unavoidably focus all up
the faculty for factors will focus all up
manufactured artifacts will focus all up

factually speaking, facts focus all up
because the facts will factual up
factual up
factual up
fact you
fact you
fact you all up

hurricane Vinny

it was a dark and starry night!
strange weather threatening
and no one to lend an ear
to the song of the satellites
singing their storm warning:

a tropical depression
gale winds gathering
suicide to stick it out
too late to evacuate!

the art of meteorology:
a science akin to astrology
reading atmospheric constellations
for visions of the future
a vane pursuit

For the art of masking our own ignorance

For the art of disguising the unknown

For the art of fabricating order from random events

For the art of forecasting fortune

For the art of forgetting our fears

For the art of finding comfort in the night

the fallout, dear Vinny
lies not with our stars
but starts with our lies

starved

I look up at the night sky
it's dark
not black
just a dark blue shade
and I see some stars
not many
just a few
some twinkle
some don't
and some have flashing lights
white
or red
maybe blue
some are fixed
some are still
some are moving across
flying objects
unidentified by me
these black sheep of the astral family
pulling the wool over my eyes
let me spell it out
letter by letter
you
half
faux
up above
how I wonder
how I do
what ever happened to the stars?
wishing mightily
upon our fall from grace . . .

ethereal

faith helium
 ballooning all out of proportion
  floating like belief in the wind
   carried away on the wings of a prayer
    soaring not a care in this world or next
     lighter than air the requiem ascending
funeral dirigible
 so goes the humanity unhindered
  upwards pitched
   spirits raised
   souls aloft
why is heaven so very high?
 not on a mountain top
 not in the stratosphere
 not in the cold, dark outer vacuum
 not above not beyond
why is heaven so very high?
 unless it is without substance?

sew lips schism

there is
no I
but I

seedless fruit

She said

O man
I will give you delight
in return
you will care for my children
take them in
give them your leavings
and waste
drop them off
wherever you like
worry not
one day they too
will bring you delight

O man
are you listening to me?

are you listening?
are you listening at all?

. . .

is there any
more selfish
than you?

iNDigNAtioN

DAmN! DAmN! DAmN!
DAmN thAt DNA, mAN!
DAmN it All, m'Am!
DAmN DAD AND mom
AND grANDpAreNts
AND ANcestors, too!
DAmN meNDeliAN meNDAcity!
DAmN trAitors
DomiNANt, AND recessive too!
A sAD legAcy!
uNwANteD iNheritANce!
coDe turNiNg to coDA!
iDeNtity DissolveD by
AciD wAsheD geNes!
we Are swept AwAy by the NucleotiDes
so very, very coNgeNiAlly
from geNerAtioN to geNerAtioN
AmeN!

so DriNk the Double helixer
AND eNter the chromozoNe
Now follow the proteAN roAD
siNgiNg
mollies
AND cules
Alive, Alive, oh!

geNie iN A bottle!
geNius up Above!
grANt us iNgenNuity!
for spAriNg geNuiNe humANity!
from DNA DAmNAtioN!

mad about scientists

you can't trust scientists!

they're always trying to take over the world, or
siding with the alien invaders because they are
a superior form of life to mere humans, or
risking the destruction of the entire universe
in their quest for truth, or playing God,
bringing down the lightning, bringing corpses
back to life, or giving animals intelligence so
that they mimic our own worst qualities while
retaining their bestial nature, or cloning
people without their knowledge, violating
their very identity, or giving themselves or
others powers that at first seem like a gift, but
ultimately prove to be more than they can
control, so they go mad or bad, or building
robots or computers with minds of their own,
whose fail-safe devices fail miserably at the
absolute worst time imaginable, or making
bombs for the military whose radiation results
in mutations, creatures threatening to wipe
out humanity in its entirety, or breeding
strains of killer insects of uncommon
intelligence, or bacteriological agents resistant
to any and all cures, or a deadly flu virus, or
one that turns people into zombies, or turning
the weather against us, unleashing killer
storms, tornadoes, hurricanes, fires, floods,
tidal waves, earthquakes, a new ice age, or a
planet so hot it's almost unlivable, or
knocking the planet out of its orbit, or
ignoring or discounting all of the warning
signs in their pursuit of forbidden knowledge,
in their lust to uncover the unknown, in trying
to know things that *man was not meant to know!*

you just can't trust scientists!

a loose carol that I like to call
"Alice Gone Noir"

Alice went to see Sam Spade
 she was decked out to the nines
she said, "I need an ace detective
 who can read between the lines"

"I'm in a deuced lot of trouble
 and there's a mystery to be solved
I can pay you double your standard rate
 long as the authorities aren't involved"

she said, "I have a broken heart"
 Sam Spade said, "welcome to the club"
his eyes drifted to her diamond rings
 he said, "Now, what's the troub—"

"it was a long time ago," she interrupted
 "a very long time ago
I was just a girl, looking for some fun
 fulfill some fantasies, you know?"

"I met an elegant chap one day
 and wound up in quite a hole—
like rabbits, you know, until I was late
 and he left with the loot that we stole"

"from the bloody queen, who was getting off
 giving head to all of the suits
and doing the humpty-dumpty while
 egging on the new recruits"

"the walrus said, 'I am appalled
 at the carpenter's glass onion song
it's all a bunch of jibber-jabber rock!
 I wonder where did we go wrong?'"

"the queen said, 'now boys, won't you play
    that fab song
that goes tweedle-de-dum-de-dee?
while I hunt down those vile criminals
 who stole my flamingos from me!'"

"I was frightened and so very alone
 things were mushrooming out of control
they tried to smoke me out like an insect
 staying free was my number one goal"

"so I made a mad dash," sweet Alice said
 "for the haberdashery store
quick as a hare, and quiet as a mouse
 I marched right in the door"

"'We have a special on bowler hats'
 the salesman said to me
'I don't think so,' I replied
 so he offered me a cup of tea"

"I took a job there, crazy as it sounds
 things started to settle down
til this cat came in with this brilliant
    smile
 I don't think that he knew how to frown"

"he took me out for a lobster dinner
 we started to get very close
I thought he was serious, til he
    disappeared
 and left me altogether morose"

"so I looked at myself in the mirror
 I said, 'girl, don't you sell yourself
    short!
stand up tall, and stop all that crying!
 you are one very fine torte!'"

"so I returned to the old haberdasher
 who said, 'marry me, Alice, my honey!'
he was madly in love with me, you see
 so I married him for the money"

"it's no wonder the police thought I did it
 when my husband turned up dead
you see, I had a reputation by then
 about being very active in bed"

"I'm an innocent girl, I tell you!
 oh, Mr. Spade, won't you take my case?"
he shuffled his feet, she looked at his
     hands
 a tear crawled down her face

"I put my cards on the table
 Is it a deal?" she asked Sam Spade
"you've had yourself quite an adventure"
    he said
 "yes, it's been quite a parade"

she said, "I've been with knaves, and I've
    been with kings
 and I've played the part of a pawn
I've gone underground, and been turned
    around
 until I wondered what planet I was on"

"your story's got more than a few holes in it"
 Sam Spade said to Alice, and sighed
"the logic is flawed, it just don't make
    sense
 babe, I can tell that you've lied"

"but I'm a sucker for a dame in distress
 lookin' for some kinda white knight
"here's to you kid, and a beautiful
    friendship"
and they walked off in the moonlight

some say they wound up in prison
 some say they went to Peru
some say they lived happily ever after
 I leave the ending up to you

at the end of the day, the mystery
 is not in who committed the crime
it's in finding coherence in a chaotic
    world
and a wonderland in our own time

criminal intent

this here rhyme
ain't worth a dime
it's a waste of time
ain't that a crime?

cursory rhymes

Little Bo Peep
has lost her sheep
she met some creep
and got in too deep
when the debt came due
all she had was ewe

Little Bo Peep
has lost her sheep
betting the daily double
she got into trouble
with a long shot tip
and now she has zip

Little Bo Peep
has lost her sheep
one of those guys
pulled the wool over her eyes
and they were out of sight
in broad daylight
skipping out like rams
legging it out on the lam
she went out of her mind
when she was unable to find
her faithless flock
she started to moan and rock
she screamed and she cursed
those sheepies were the worst

Little Bo Peep
has lost her sheep
to another pastor
a religious broadcaster
they couldn't resist
that ol' televangelist
like birds of a feather
in search of fair weather
they flocked to the new shepherd
a born again leopard
thought they spotted a winner
but he had them for dinner

Little Bo Peep
has lost her sheep
she left them a loan
mortgaged her home
to be an entrepreneur
selling manure
as fertilizer
now she's poorer but wiser

Little Bo Peep
has lost her mutton
she blamed Willie Sutton
put a gun to his head
shot that bank robber dead
they called it a crime of passion
now she's modeling, after a fashion

Little Bo Peep
has lost her lamb
so she bought a web cam
now she rakes in the dough
and you know where those sheep can go

Little Bo Peep
has lost her sheep
now she can't sleep
she's an insomniac
ain't that whack
to get her life in order
she moved south of the border
and started counting llama
now she's a grande dama

Little Bo Peep
has lost her sheep
to Little Bo Duke
and his cousin Luke
playing Texas Hold 'em
didn't know when to fold 'em
the boys lost their way
with those beasts, so they say
so they left them alone
to wander on home
wagging their tails behind them

ode on a geekian turn

if Luke Skywalker had not blown up
the death star
then the rebels would have been crushed
the empire would have reigned supreme
Yoda would have gone to his grave as
the last Jedi
and Darth Vader would never have been
redeemed
the emperor's iron fist would have stifled
the exploration of galaxies far, far away
so that a long, long time later
no life would have migrated to
planet earth
no human beings would have been present
to build cities and civilizations
there would be no scientific discoveries
or new inventions
no rockets to outer space
no walking on the moon
and centuries from now
there would be no warp drive
or transporters
no Starship Enterprise
no Captain Kirk
no Mr. Spock
the half-human, half-Vulcan hybrid
no United Federation of Planets
no one to stand against
the Klingons
the Romulans
the Dominion and
the Borg

thank goodness the Force was with us then

is it with us now?

St. O'Nes tones to nest one

rolling along, we gather no moss
but frankly, we don't think it any great loss
for us, it's like having a fungus infection
we'll keep on rolling, in any direction

if we don't keep on rolling, we'll wind up
    being turned
by folks who're searching, and haven't yet
    adjourned
they're looking everywhere, putting up such
    a fuss
those bigoted bastards, always suspecting us

the first of our kind, he shall go nameless
he was pure of heart, and utterly blameless
so why in the world was he the one to be cast?
we'll keep living in sin, at least then we'll last

take a hit from a head, and we may get high
but falling from great heights, we will not die
still, we may mark the grave of some
    unfortunate soul
who is no longer healthy, nor hearty, nor
    whole!

we're cold, it's true, but it don't mean we're
    dead
we're weights, that's true too, but we ain't
    made from lead
we mark a short distance, 'cause we can't be
    thrown far
and we'll remain sober, even sitting at the bar

if you're looking for blood, we've none to give
the kidneys, now there's a place we can live
we can make up a heart, though we haven't a
	cell
a hard heart without heart, that's a tale you
	can tell

you can put us in soup, but you know you
	can't eat us
we are very concrete, you'll never defeat us
we're stubborn as walls, and we're cobblers of
	roads
we're too heavy for you, you can't carry our
	loads

we'll break your bones, and make it stick
we'll kill two birds, if we're quick
we'll kill a goliath, if we're well slung
and we can kill you too, when we're flung

so, we're hiding out in our safe house tonight
it's made out of glass, we hide in plain sight
and nobody dares throw us out, we're steady
	and strong
come daybreak, we'll move on, keep rolling
	along

without a home and completely unknown
without an address, without even a phone
taking our show on the road, and paying our
	dues
playing in the band, pumped up rhythm and
	blues

(everybody's doin' the)
danse macabre

when the dead come out to play
it will be a happy day
and we all will shout hurray
and sing and dance

we will joke and fool around
laugh so hard we hit the ground
and we'll make a merry sound
and wet our pants

when the dead come out to sing
the bells will toll and ring
and we'll have a crazy fling
and act insane

we will jump up, up, and down
skip the loo and go to town
shed tears of joy to make us drown
and feel no pain

when the dead come out to stroll
it will gladden every soul
gathering on the grassy knoll
for the party

we will drink grain alcohol
tripping lightly we will fall
and we'll toast them one and all
hell and hearty

when the dead come out to strut
you will feel it in your gut
that you'll make the final cut
to go join them

go and march in their parade
go and join their masquerade
be part of their escapade
and their mayhem

when the dead come out to dine
we will drink our finest wine
and we'll form a conga line
from here to there

they are hungry, that we know
we will feed them as we go
cooked or raw, friend or foe
they just don't care

when the dead come out to kiss
every mister and every miss
that abyss will bring us bliss
and excitement

wedding bells are in the air
when the foul join with the fair
wearing flowers, if they have hair
they're heaven sent

when the dead come out to love
put on stockings and a glove
they're a gift from up above
can you feel it?

they will take you in their arms
you'll surrender to their charms
you'll ignore all the alarms
there's no exit

when the dead come out to dance
we'll give in to the romance
ecstasy when we have the chance
to be as one

joyful jig or waltzing glide
there'll be nowhere you can hide
and when everyone has died
oh, we'll have fun

danse macabre for a night
danse macabre 'til morning light
danse macabre to give you the fright
of all your days

danse macabre at the hop
danse macabre and never stop
danse macabre until you drop
sing purple haze

danse macabre for a thrill
danse macabre if you will
danse macabre get your fill
the latest craze

what I do

I ex therefore I am
I ax 'em
nicely first
but thoreauly
alone in isolation
I act my part
this ex-ham in nation
ask me I am

a Halloween holiday getaway
(to the Transylvanian Alps)

come, take the time
and we will climb
up the Transylvanian Alps
and we will dine
on fresh blood wine
and a *ghoulash* made of scalps

and if you please
then bring your skis
and we'll take in the slopes
for the folk below
seeing us on the snow
will *crush* all of their hopes

we'll hear their shrieks
as we fly from the peaks
like hawks hunting their prey
we'll dive and we'll soar
we'll let out a *roar*
and the peasants shall know dismay

we'll come out at night
on the mountains so white
speckled with drops of red!
like *paprika* spice
on a bed of rice
we'll sleep soundly once we've fed

from Budapest
to Bucharest
Austria, Hungary, and Rumania
there's no resort
for our *cohort*
like the Alps of Transylvania!*

**Packages begin at US$666. Taxes not included. May be subject to additional charges. Ski & quisling rental offered for a nominal fee. Some restrictions may apply. Not liable for loss or injury due to exposure to sunlight, wooden stake, religious articles, garlic, silver bullet, or Van Helsing. Based on availability.*

come (a dark summoning)

come to me forbidden
come to me, my taste
come to me, my dark storm cloud
come to me in haste

come to me in madness
come to me in chains
come to me like lightning strikes
come like acid rains

come to me in shadow
come to me, my flood
come to me, my pestilence
come to me in blood

come, my conflagration
come, fall into my trance
come, perform your ululations
come, do your serpent's dance

come to me, my blackest depths
come, my sharp-toothed shark
come to me, my carrion sweet
come, my spider dark

come to me unbitten
come, surrender to my spell
come to me, my sphinx supine
come, bring me waters from your well

come to me, my cauldron brew
come to me, red rum
come to me, my chthonic boom
come to me now come

root

colorless as night, creature of the dark
darkening the sky, blotting out the light
lightning in reverse, without shine or spark
sparkling feathered black, flying in the night
night that never ends, no escape from fear
fearing shadows cover, fearing the fall
falling into cold embrace, she draws near
nearing dark flame's hot breath, now forced to
    crawl
crawl now without sight, and without a will
willing surrender to the emptiness
emptying self to give the dark its fill
filling the void with self, and so to bless
bless the consummation and its dark fruit
fruit and flowers exist not without root

undone

and so, I am...
  but hold...
my word!
my shoelace has come...
  whoa...
    ow!
      ow!
       ow!
        ow!
         ow!

wyrm spit

I have grown monstrous with age
expansive in power
but there is no disguising
the skin of my crimes
and yet
I still forget myself
and wonder why you
recoil from my touch
I reach for you
as you shake and cry
your beauty moves me
to my very depths
I would devour you whole
it's not for the taste
but only to fill
the hollow spaces inside
I expect no sympathy from you
as your prayers to escape my sight
go unanswered
I remain
stretching
strangling
do not struggle
there is no salvation
there is only
salivation

a warning

There are colors I have known [2]that I cannot name, [3]that I cannot tell apart, [4]that all that can be said of them is, [5]they are wrong. [6]There are colors that are not native to this time and place, [7]to this earth and sea and sky, [8]colors that ought not to exist, [9]colors that are uncaring, uncanny, and unclean, [10]colors that are dissonant and noisome, [11]colors that blaspheme and violate, [12]colors that defile and desecrate, [13]colors that pain and pierce and stab the eye, [14]colors that are tainted and cursed, [15]that open doors that can never again be closed. [16]Paint your walls with these colors, [17]and evil will dwell with you. [18]Kiss a woman lipsticked with these colors, [19]and none shall hear from you again. [20]Look at lights displaying these colors, [21]and you will lose your sight, and sanity. [22]For every color that you know, [23]there is a shade that is ugly and unnatural, [24]there is a shade that is hostile and devouring, [25]there is a shade that was never meant to be. [26]Be mindful, be watchful, be wary. [27]Be warned.

clinched

the Queen Bee
broadcasts her pheromones
transmits her message
send in the drones

once summoned
the drone must come
no choice but to obey
none wanted
she is the Queen
her will be done

a prisoner of biology
is all he will ever be
eyes wide open he
is trapped quite willingly
no escape   no desire to be free

one shot at love
the time of his *life*
ecstasy...
then *agony*!
to bee...
then *not to bee*
clinch...
then *crunch*

no point praying, man, 'tis over
no witnesses to speak of
only the black widow spied her

the mating habits
of the bees are for the birds
but wherever you go
and whatever you do
and whoever you may be
it's always the same:
to be a man
is *hard*!

some call it love

I admire your skills
said the fly to the spider
your architecture's second to none

the fly flashed a smile
you're an artiste my dear
he waxed eloquent
an author par excellence
he spoke seductively
your creativity's without compare
adding
I see beauty and truth in all your designs
whispering now
I am awestruck
and rendered
blind, deaf and dumb
to all else
by your
brilliance extraordinaire

the spider gave the fly
a quite curious look
as she spun from on high
coming down
she was laughing quietly
just to herself
and was heard
to exclaim sweetly
yum!

more cursory rhymes

Little Jack Horner
sat in the corner
eating his christmas pie
all the rest were in fear of him
no one could get near of him
else he'd stick his thumb in their eye

Little Jack Horner
sat in the corner
eating his octopi
he would trade his ferrari
for a plate of calamari
saying, *what a gourmet am I*

Little Jack Horner
sat in the corner
trying to calculate pi
he said, *it's quite an endeavor*
seems to go on forever
I'll be doing this 'til the day I die

Little Jack Horner
stood on a street corner
singing doo-wop a cappella
people tossed coins in his hat
as he sang his best scat
and he said, I am a talented fella

Little Jack Horner
went to a neutral corner
while the ref counted to ten
Joe Palooka stayed down
took a dive, then left town
making Jack welterweight champion

Little Jack Horner
said he tried to warn her
to keep her pie hole shut
the judge said, *no way
you'll see the light of day*
and gave him life without you know what

Little Jack Horner
sat in the corner
said, I won't be an informer
no, *I won't be no snitch
and wind up in a ditch
I ain't no dirty rat
and that, my friend, is that*

Little Jack Horner
sat at the coroner
to identify the body
of his boss, John Gotti
Gotti was Jack's capo
now he's taking a permanent napo

Little Jack Horner
was just another mourner
at the mafia funeral
lacking all repentance
he vowed to have vengeance
and off his enemies, one and all

Little Jack Horner
hid in the corner
then ran downtown
to Chinatown
after going mano-a-mano
with Tony Soprano
he thought he could take on the boss
but Tony turned him into plum sauce

Little Jack Horner
had no use for a foreigner
there wasn't any doubt
he wanted to throw them all out
and build a wall around the border
he said that we must have order
ethnic cleansing was his game
racial purity by another name
he caused quite a furor
over whose blood was purer
he thought he was quite plum
but he was just plain dumb

Little Jack Horner
had a woman, but scorned her
in case you're curious
yes, she was quite furious
she gave him hell
down the stairs he fell
an accident, if you please
or so she told the authorities

Little Jack Horner
worked for Time-Warner
was a media mogul
and that's no bull
he made a movie
thought everything was groovy
but it went over budget
no way he could fudge it
and it was a big flop
saw the profit margins drop
he said, *what a good boy am I*
now he works in a diner, serving pie

Little Jack Horner
sat in the corner
while the water level rose
he said, *what a bummer*
and called in a plumber
who promptly shut off the garden hose

Little Jack Horner
thumbed his nose at you all
plumbed the depths of the stall
'til he heard a great hush
then he decided to flush
and said, What a good boy am I

as the stars grow cross (disBard)

he breaks a lighthouse window, and says, I'm
a soft touch, my jewel, it's Easter Sunday and
I'm mooning over you

she answers, you are artful as you roam from
me, oh, you may wear your denial like a
nametag, but I refuse to part my thighs
farther, for now, sorry, sweet thing, but I'm
partying without you, at least until tomorrow

sniff

someone's counting noses
someone's winning by a nose
someone's nose is out of joint
someone's nose is hard
someone's got his nose to the grindstone
someone's paying through the nose
someone's looking down his nose
someone's looking right under his nose
someone's nose is taking a dive
someone's turning his nose up
someone's nose is up in the air
someone's keeping his nose clean
someone's rubbing his nose in it
someone's being led around by the nose
someone's cut off his nose to spite his face
someone's a nosy-parker
someone's got a nose for news
someone's nosing around
someone's sticking his nose
      where it don't belong
someone's too damn nosy for his own good
but a nose by any other name
      would smell as sweet!

the hunters' love

mistress of wolves

                      rises at dusk

to find her pack once more

           and they dance their union
         we are one   *we are one*
        and they sing their communion
        we are legion   *we are legion*
           we are all of us
           all of us are we
             we are we
              we are

the hunters' love

    is fierce and hungry
    is full and relentless
    is faithful and unyielding

          the stars spasm in envy
         we look on with desire
           but who can grasp
             or touch
           or even approach

                 who can know the hunters' love?

genesis

to learn how to speak
one must first learn how to listen
in communication as in procreation
conception follows reception

interdiction

please don't interrupt me
and correct the way I talk
you pronounce your words
the way you want to
and I'll speak in a voice of my own
yes thank you very much
for your concern but
I'll speak in a voice of my own

the blind guitarist

Son to Homer
he calls out
  Sing O Muse!

Son to Justitia
with an ear for an eye

no vision to mislead him or to confuse
only hearing divides the truth from the lie

getting an earfuel

the aura of the oral
is colored like the coral
and it's aural to the core
where it's all oil or it's all coal

meanderthal

stirred to wandering the shape
    of polyphonic glory
moved to winding wonder along
    roughly contoured paths
following science of the foot
    in circuitry oblique

guided by the lonely breath
    of unseen spirit living
sounding out the form
    of this humble, rust-hued earth
soft spoken maps of vanished moments
    each with harmonies unique

all she rote

reckless recall
dismembered memory
wracked & abandoned
fragmented flashes
reminders remanded
recollect
retain and retrieve

the white

we cannot abide the white for very long
it's just not in our nature
to accept the empty canvas slate or space
we feel compelled
to leave our mark on the blankness
a footprint
a handprint
a line
a trace
a sign that says
I was
I am
I will be
beyond what is
more than
pictures
words
names
leave a piece of ourselves
against the promise of erasure
that is the white

words fail

they always do. but never more than now. only
joining voices. to cry upon the wind. echoing
the sounds. of shattered hearts.

the butterfly affect

Frida floating free
callow folk don't understand how
color can hide
the tragic loss. life's fortunes
can be fuel for lightening
the fire that burns
within. a glow that warms the puppet stage
you built. only fools forget how to play
with dolls. let them act out a drama you
cannot live. let them tell
the story of your
heart. the fetal beat of
withering futility. there
is no perfect symmetry. in this
life or the next.

beware the ideologies of Mocks. beware the
common ground. no safety in dictatorships
of the pedestrian who strolls
or trots or runs. no
cure in pull of gravity.

listen to the song of
butterflies that only you can
hear. a chorale of wings that
cannot be contained by
broken limns. their breath a
wind that amplifies the inner voice. and who
can stand against the gale? let it take
you away from pain. smoke becomes one with
clouds above while the ashes that remain
cast shadows of longing. pieces of
a life we use to
solve a puzzle that
can never be. we dig and sift and can
never see how she is
finally   finally
              floating free

iconography

the bell rings
the dagger flies
no one suspected the ballerina
the man in the business suit looked on

    though we are divided
    you are my mirror image

he said

    we must watch and wash each other
    separated as we are
    how else to read the signs?
    except up close and in fine detail?
    fine detail indeed!

each one goes to his/her room
his/her room
yes his/her room
each one goes to his/her room
and you know the rest

ash-Tray

ig-Pay
atin-Lay
is-way
an-way
easy-way
ay-way
o-tay
ake-may
a-way
yme-rhay,

ut-bay
is-way
it-way
art-way
or-way
is-way
it-way
ash-tray?

course

silly bus
follow the route paved with syllables
travel by word
beware sell abuse
buyer beware cell abyss
please... don't... get... lost...

a reading from the Book of M

And it came to pass
   that a Messenger
    came to deliver a message
   and the message was delivered
    by the Messenger.

And it came to pass
   that a Prophet foretold
   that a Messenger would come
    to deliver a Message
   and the Message was delivered
    by the Messenger
   as the Prophet foretold.

And it came to pass
   that a Priest prayed
   that a Prophet would foretell
   that a Messenger would come
    to deliver a Message
   and the Message was delivered
    by the Messenger
   as the Prophet foretold
   as the Priest prayed.

And it came to pass
   that a King commanded
   that a Priest would pray
   that a Prophet would foretell
   that a Messenger would come
    to deliver a Message
   and the Message was delivered
    by the Messenger
   as the Prophet foretold
   as the Priest prayed
   as the King commanded.

And it came to pass
    that a Scribe wrote
    that a King would command
    that a Priest would pray
    that a Prophet would foretell
    that a Messenger would come
      to deliver a Message
    and the Message was delivered
      by the Messenger
    as the Prophet foretold
    as the Priest prayed
    as the King commanded
    as the Scribe wrote.

And it came to pass
    that a Message was sent
    that a Scribe would write
    that a King would command
    that a Priest would pray
    that a Prophet would foretell
    that a Messenger would come
      to deliver a Message
    and the Message was delivered
      by the Messenger
    as the Prophet foretold
    as the Priest prayed
    as the King commanded
    as the Scribe wrote
    so was sent the Message.

writ large

the written word
is so absurd
it's seen but not heard
it can be blurred
but not slurred

once written twice shy
sounds marching off to die
and no one left to answer why
just follow in formation
for you and eye

yes follow the script
  you have no choice
yes stay true to type
  face it without voice
yes focus and fixate
  in vision rejoice
yes establish silence
  and eliminate noise

turn speech into stone
petrify flesh and bone
freeze rhythm and tone

belief becomes black and white
and justice colorblind
love and beauty are framed
between covers to bind
up our passions and
on the shelf store our mind

and our prison comes from a pen
and our sentence written once again
and the law of the letter
  rules women and men
blank page is our womb
finished tome is our tomb

epitaph

I am but a memory
of what once was alive
and given a choice
I would be living still
so perhaps it is best
that the choice is not mine
perhaps it is best
perhaps
perhaps
but all that is left
is a trace, a reflection
an echo, a fossil, a ruin
if I could, I'd be with you
to talk it all over
hear your thoughts and opinions
but this is all that is left
I am sorry to say
there is no dying without living
of that we are certain
and so then it follows
that in living we're dying
in life there is death
but between the two there are words
there are words
between the two there are words

boustrophedon

I am the alpha to your omega babe
one number in first am I
I am your baby blue aleph babe
none to second am I

I am mighty I am muscular
strength and stamina am I
I pull and pull with all my power
length entire the pull I

my back is strong here I come with my load
day after day rows making
I move the earth to sow my seed
obey must I and yoked am I

I am harnessed but no hoe
beat to swords your again come
I scratch your ditch in the dirt and soil
street long straight my digging

but I go both ways and that's a fact
know will you and me monitor
I zig and zag and zig again
go I right left right left

I make my marks for all to see
back and forth and back going
I write my earthy poetry
knack the got have I know you

unsaid words

silent on the page they patiently sit
all lined up quietly row by row bound
taking queues from eyeteeth sowed in the
    ground
straight truly forming a most perfect fit
passive, complacent, breathless, they
    don't mind
they show no anger at their voiceless
    plight
they don't complain that their world's
    black and white
they ask for nothing, their world is
    aligned
they wait for their time, they wait for
    their chance
they are filled with potential energy
they are wallflowers waiting for a dance
they are prisoners waiting for a key
they are lovers waiting for a romance
they wait for you and me to set them free

again and again

I see Alexander's city burning
the great metropolis of learning
    is consumed

I hear the cries of
    pyrrhic victory
the war against papyrus has been won

the crowd cheering
    chanting
dancing
    in red delight
as smoke erases the stars

and
ashes fall to the waters
blackening reflection
for all time . . .

the dark closes in
hot winds assailing
transported in the firestorm
no safe harbor
for scholarship

the flames are on the waters
the waters of
memory
    and muse . . .

knowledge bleeds
and wisdom turns
    to vapor
barbs on bare skin pierce
drawing crimson flickerings
but no atonement
        or affliction
            can restore what now is gone

I see the torch ignited by
blistered pride
rashes of passion
varicose vanities
trust grown feeble and rusted
reckless betrayal, a murder
    of legacy and birthright
as acid adders and asps spit their
    arsonic poison—

and the tears of reading eyes
    are too few
to extinguish
    the propagating vampyres
as they feast on urbs of healing

cry out the lamentations:

lost
lost forever
an end
an end
to Aristotelian vision
to Macedonian dream
to Ptolemian labor
to Cleopatrian love
to Alexandrian light

but in the fires of despair
I hear the sound of wings
Minerva's owl takes flight

somewhere

somewhere

somewhere

a new home awaits . . .

the princess of Nepal

the princess of Nepal
journeyed so very far
arriving at the door
of the library

over mountains at war with the stars
   her hair an obsidian spring
across honeyed, swarming sands
   her skin a banyan polished most fine
past floods that rip and claw at the land
   her face proliferate poppies afield
through winds that melt down solid stone
   her hands twin parakeets at play
around chasms that seduce the ignoble
   her will and her vision her fame

the princess of Nepal
journeyed so very far
such a long, long way to come
to come to read a book

chirography

The old man in the scriptorium
sat at his carrel and copied
the ancient manuscript
dried and brittle with age
letter by letter
word by word
sentences resounding over centuries
handwritten memories coming to mind
dreaming, as he wrote...

    I dip my pen
    into your inkwell
    and sign my name
    in strokes long, hard, and bold
    my goose quill quivers
    as I leave my mark
    on your soft, smooth vellum
    I am your scribe
    my calligraphy illuminates
    your tightly bound codex
    a colophonic ending
    to another session of copying
    reproduction without replication
    a ritual repeated with variation
    puritanical types
    call it corruption
    not recognizing a labor of love
    a carnal craft
    the most intimate of encounters
    two minds becoming one
    thoughts tracing patterns
    for the eye to see
    words working into flesh
    worlds waiting to be reborn...

the old man smiled
and snored...

lettered

putting pen to paper
in personal expression
pressing down hard
and harder still
I make my mark
imprinting myself on surface memory

oh but my narcissism breeds
your narcolepsy
and it's all narcheology now

cramped and crimped
clumsy handed ballpoints
stab puncture rip and tear
wounded words pour through the gash
splattering the white expanse
dark blots pool across thin blue lines
begging to be read

ink stained fingers give me away
the prints match
you realize
you see the guilt smudged on my face
and recognize the signature
left on the remains
as my own

the letters are dead
and I am imprisoned
enveloped by these walls
praying for freedom
redemption and deliverance
but where else
can I address
my desire?
I plead with you
do not
stamp me out

my crafty hand never mastered the art
of pure penmanship
I couldn't follow the script
you wrote out for me
I lacked the dexterity
to handle your sensuality
I couldn't calibrate your graphical touch
I longed for the beauty
of your lines and curves
but the pleasure of your art
proved elliptically elusive

yet my tripod pinch
roused you from dreams
to a curious awakening
tips tapped the key
to your type of delight
rough and drafty and maybe
a little bit crude

and so I came to wallow in my own
dis-cursive carvings and cravings
leaving bits and pieces of me behind
a trail of crumbs
for you to follow if you want
for I can never find my way back
the lines only go
left to right and
top to bottom and
page to page and
step by step by step
I send
descend and
ascend up
side down
convey   express
note down
record
put out
and then
pass on

brother John

morning bells are ringing
brother John is sleeping
lazy little monk he
had too much to drink
last night and now it seems that he
is late for morning prayers
bound to raise some hairs
upon the elder's pate
or maybe just a split
about how many angels
can be piled upon his plate
breakfast serving cake
he eats his fill of food
and then goes back for more
brown ale to wash it down
again the bells are ringing
but he lingers with his meal
ignores the elder's frown he's
in no hurry to move on
to go to work with pen and ink
on parchment pages thick
draws a unicorn whose head and horn
rest along a virgin's lap
and his thoughts drift down
through memories of maidens
pretty girls that he once knew
who brought on deep inside him
stirrings of the... heart
visions that still visit him
each and every night
that come to him in dreams
delightful reveries
and oh how he hates the sound
when morning bells are ringing
ding! ding! dong!
ding! ding! dong!

left hand lover

Leonardo left hand lover
loved his Venus of the waters
loved her city of the people
loved her people of the city
crafts and commerce
carnival knowledge
lovers crossing on the water
across her city
boats and bridges
left hand lover Leonardo
built machines fantastical
to fortify
to float and fly
for his lover
he had no other
he sent her notes in secret writing
of his vision
of her beauty
lonely lover Leonardo
left hand lover's lonely life
left her city
left his lover
left alone
there was no other
Leonardo left hand lover

yo! yo! Johann!
Mainz your own business

goody goody
Gutenberg
we're all so very impressed
with your moves
you're so able
we know your type
you leave your imprint
on all that you do
copy that
copy that
copy that
copy that
copy that
copy that
copy that
copy that
modern times begin with you

print

aw, Thor!
aw, Thor!
steam powers presses like thunder
cop he writes
or play jurist
trial and errata
off set and type cast ink

one six one one

James was the first
to come down from the north
thereby proving the theorem
that six into one yields three thirds

James came down from the north
to declare that a divine write
  be commissioned
to be assembled by committee
committed to the service
of God and country
together as one
a concerted effort

and what did
he brew
with this
stew art
of his?

James made magic
on the vernacular equinox
a translation
of spiritual force
a spell to cast
upon all who share
the tongue of angles
an enchantment
working with the word
Eve writ
a sacred wedding
to bless and
to enrich his realm
forevermore

our plague days

A *plague*! A *plague*!
Of *plagiarism*!
A pox upon our house!
A noxious pox of chicken scratch!
A literary apocalypse!
Fifth horseman riding roughshod
over fourth estate!
Trespassers on intellectual property!
Transgressors eschewing all decency!
With your *insincerest* form of flattery!
And your crimes of dispassion!
Dispatched with dishonesty!
Prosper not, base cheats
and ne'er-do-wells!
Stealing sentences!
Robbing phrases!
Purloining expression!
With such contemptuous disease!
Thieves in the digital night!
With your evil tools of cut and paste!
Word-burglars with your *copywrongs*!
Absconding scoundrels!
You are our affliction!
Outcast dispel this foul air
of derivation!
This contagion that eschews all quotation!
Vile pestilence that you are!
I wish you *Damnation*!

But hold
These lines came to me in a fever
But now a chill attacks my spine
Are these words that I have penned
  truly mine?
Or did I stumble 'pon them
  in some grave tome?
Digging about late one night
  in times long past away?

Now half-remembered,
  now half-dismembered?
Be it ale or ailment, might I be
  under the influence?
O, the anxiety! Sweet muse
  grant me certainty...

Aha! I have it! To insure that nothing
unoriginal issues forth from my mouth or
hand, I shall henceforth communicate in a
language entirely of my own devising
known only to me!

ntp okbftd czxr

Z *okzftd*! Z *okzftd*!
Ne *okzfhzqhrl*!
Z onw tonm ntq gntrd!
Z mnwhntr onw ne bghbjdm rbqzsbg!
Z khsdqzqx zonbzkxord!
Ehesg gnqrdlzm qhchmf qntfgrgnc
Nudq entqsg drszsd!
Sqdrozrrdqr nm hmsdkkdbstzk oqnodqsx!
Sqzmrfqdrrnqr drbgdvhmf zkk cdbdmbx!
Vhsg xntq *hmrhmbdqdrs* enql ne ekzssdqx!
Zmc xntq bqhldr ne chrozrrhnm!
Chrozsbgdc vhsg chrgnmdrsx!
Oqnrodq mns, azrd bgdzsr
zmc md'dq-cn-vdkkr!
Rsdzkhmf rdmsdmbdr!

Qnaahmf ogqzrdr!
Otqknhmhmf dwoqdrrhnm!
Vhsg rtbg bnmsdlostntr chrdzrd!
Sghdudr hm sgd chfhszk mhfgs!
Vhsg xntq duhk snnkr ne bts zmc ozrsd!
Vnqc-atqfkzqr vhsg xntq *bnoxvqnmfr*!
Zarbnmchmf rbntmcqdkr!
Xnt zqd ntq zeekhbshnm!
Ntsbzrs chrodk sghr entk zh
ne cdqhuzshnm!
Sghr bnmszfhnm sgzs drbgdvr
zkk ptnszshnm!
Uhkd odrshkdmbd sgzs xnt zqd!
H vhrg xnt *Czlmzshnm*!

Ats gnkc!
Tgdrd khmdr bzld sn ld hm z edudq!
Ats mnv z bghkk zsszbjr lx rohmd!
Zqd sgdrd vnqcr sgzs h gzud odmmdc
   sqtkx lhmd?
Nq chc H rstlakd 'onm sgdl
   hm rnld fqzud snld?
Chffhmf zants kzsd nmd mhfgs
   hm shldr knmf ozrrdc zvzx?
Mnv gzke-qdldladqdc, mnv gzke-chrldladqdc?
Ad hs zkd nq zhkldms, lhfgs H ad
   tmcdq sgd hmektdmbd?
N, sgd zmwhdsx! Rvdds ltrd
   fqzms ld bdqszhmsx!

Zgz! H gzud hs! Sn hmrtqd sgzs mnsghmf
tmnqhfhmzk hrrtdr enqsg eqnl lx lntsg nq
gzmc, H rgzkk gdmbdenqsg bnlltmhbzsd hm z
kzmftzfd dmshqdkx ne lx nvm cduhrhmf
jmnvm nmkx sn ld!

90

stimulus-response theory

won't you stop kneejerking me around?

    I'm off to buy a book
        to book a fare
        to fare thee well
        to well and good
        to good and bye
        to bye and buy
            a book
        to write your name in

    so I can blot it out!

writer's shock

don't worry
don't worry
there are always more pages to fill
you won't run out of space
you will only run out of time

pen

ultimate
knife
name
light
sill
chant
ants
shun
umbra
kneeless
net trait
knit tents
tag gone
men ship
null tee
null eyes

haunting (a high boo)

there but not not there
presence of absence not absent of presence
being not being being not

train I ride, 16 coaches long

01. I point my finger and you know
    what I mean

02. the sounds I make are echoing

03. my handprint on the wall

04. our rituals of memory, your
    theater of words

05. my tokens of accounting

06. their aura of the aural

07. I see signs of each
    syllable, you reduce it
    all to consonance

08. we take vowels of silence

09. they copy us again again

10. I press the point and you tell me
    all about your type

11. we date ourselves again again

12. I page the preface, you reach
    the climax

13. I take pictures again again

14. you are moved by the sequence

15. they run cables all around us

16. we are swept up by the current
    and are gone

no remorse

there was an age
    when the wires sang
    with buzzes and beeps
      both short and long
          dah-di-dit dah-dah-dah dah di-di-dit
                – •• – – – – •••

back and forth the electric
    alphabet rang
    like church bells playing
      a mighty song
            dah-di-dit di-dah di-di-dit
            di-di-di-dit dit di-di-dit
        – •• •– ••• •••• • •••

there was an age
    when the airwaves hummed
    the spectrum filled
      with unearthly tones
      dah-dah dah-dah-dah di-dah-dit di-di-dit dit
           – – – – – •–• •••• •

through the skies above
    the rhythms thummed
    with ethereal
      ghostly moans
        dah-di-dah-dit dah-dah-dah dah-di-dit dit
           – •–• – – – –•• •

operators played
    their magnetic keys
    keeping the beat
      with style and flair
            dah dit di-dah-di-dit dit
              – • •–•• •
            dah-dah-dit di-dah-dit di-dah
            di-dah-dah-dit di-di-di-dit
          – –• •–• •– •––• ••••

across the continent
        and overseas
        sending their messages
            with skill and care
                        di-dah-dah di-dit di-dah-dit dit
                            • — —   • •   • — •   •

                    di-dah-di-dit dit di-di-dit di-di-dit
                        • — • •   •   • • •   • • •

from Maine to Texas
        and beyond
        great distances bridged
            at a speed sublime
                        dit di-dit dah-dah-dit di-di-di-dit
                            •   • •   — — •   • • • •

                        dah dit dit dah-dit
                            —   •   •   — •

uniting us all
        in a common bond
        one neighborhood
            out of space and time
                        di-di-dah-dit dah-dah-dah
                    di-dah-dit dah dah-di-dah-dah
                    • • — •   — — —   • — •   —   — • — —
                        di-di-dah-dit dah-dah-dah
                            di-di-dah di-dah-dit
                    • • — •   — — —   • • —   • — •

    and now new songs
        fill the atmosphere
        and travel along wires
            that encircle the Earth
                        di-di-dit di-dah dah-dah
                    di-di-dah dit di-dah-di-dit
                    • • •   • —   — —   • • —   •   • — • •

but listening hard
        you still can hear
        the binary tune
            from that moment of birth
                dah-dah dah-dah-dah di-dah-dit di-di-dit dit
                    — —   — — —   • — •   • • •   •

electric shocker

of kites and keys
dead legs of frogs
catch fire in a bottle
direct the life force
in lines and circles
break silences with music
ignite the countless tiny suns
stitch them together in galaxies
be present in all places
be always ever absent
be at one and apart
be everyone and no one
be alone within a crowd
be all powerful and nothingness
bring an end to memory and pain
and bring a new start
   to an ailing and stilled heart

meatless

I sail the electric sea
like my angel sails the aether
escaping earth's gravity
she never looks beneath her

always almost something there

always almost something there
all ways all or most of the sum
  of things here or there
there are things some most or
  all of them away with them all
something there almost always
some things all or mostly always there
away with them all these things that
  some most of all appear to be there
always almost real touching
  something there
something kissing reality there
  most of all all ways and means
what the word means means
something really there face of
  almost already always
ready almost always interfacing
  something there
always already almost touching
  sum of all things there between
between among pervade surround around
really ready everywhere the same
always almost something there

Marconi Mussolini

Marconi Mussolini
Marconi Mussolini
macabre moose a-leanin' towerin'
pizza pasta pesto
cookin' up a feast to serve
stir the pot and carve the meat
right off the bone

speakin' power to the truth
radiate waves and you salute
send out signals
roamin' empires of the air

enter homes when you want to
without warrant or a welcome
rule the skies and seas the land
devoted to devourin'
macaroni tortellini

Mercury Maserati
fashion a faster brighter future
lighting up the atmosphere
explosions in the making
bursting out of shelled containments
flashing out into the night
marionette Marinetti
lighting strikes and all are singing
hail storm
true persons
hail
Marc Antony muscleman

Marconi mausoleum
Marconi mausoleum
fetish figura
birds of a feather
sticks tied together
bound and bundled
rods to rule you

grantin' axes their power
poles runnin' north and south
birds of a fetter
tethered together
by glamour galvanized
by charisma magnetized
by desire electrified

Marc one and Marc only
Marc uno not Marc dué
no never the twain shall meet

who calls you from the ether?
who calls you from on high?
who calls you now to service?
as you leave your
mark on history
whose voice will master you?

afar

you fill me with love from afar
at home
at work
in my car
though I don't know where the hell
you are
you fill me with love from afar

out, out brief candle

I reached for the remote
turned on the TV
nothing particular was on
so I just started zapping around
looking for something
to distract my attention
pass the time away
with these shadows
that play upon the screen
bits and pieces of stories
that walk on and off the stage
as con artists
take their 30-second struts
and news artists
give their half-a-minute frets
and mysterious messages
creep along the bottom
and off again into the dusty void
tomorrow and tomorrow it will be the same
schizophrenic syllables and
signs of nothingness
furious sounds and idiots
chasing their own tales
and moving lights to lure and
play us for fools
make an end of it
turn the damnéd thing right off
yesterday evaporates
the hour is late
I must pace myself
there's a new day about to dawn
Good TiVO! Kind DVR!
allow me to escape this living death
and save me to the end
of recorded time

and that's the way it is

and that's the way it is.
they shout their warning:
Low water! Low water!
to no avail...
the ship has run aground
sands have barred your way
they say, *this far, and no further.*

and that's the way it is.
when fiduciary strains filled the air
and the sure-handed steersman
summoned and dismissed
the gods and demons of the day...
now the evening meal is over
and the long night thins the air

and that's the way it is.
as one ritual bleeds into another
breaking bread and news and earth
our father now in heaven
how hollow are the men and women who
followed in your wake
false-faced, fair-featured and unbalanced
minds, unmeasured
punch drunkards who have
replaced report with retort
and trust with the bluster of fools.

and that's the way it is.
seabee essence...
adjourn nihilism...
Low water! Low water!
goodbye, night chronicler, you can
sail high to the stars now, and
steer clear of this angry, noisy age...
sail high to the stars now...
and that's   the way   it is.

television interview

and
they jeered
because she took the trouble
to put her makeup on
to fix her hair
to dress up
to look her best
for the cameras

but
who
can judge how we face
such a devastating loss

but
who
can measure
and prescribe our grief

but
who
can know our pain
and how we should respond

but
who
can make demands
of our sorrow
?

in the age of show business

in memory of Neil Postman

the medium is a mess, aging us
  from childhood to adulthood at the speed of light
  from zero to sixty overnight

wind burn transforming us
  from raw to cooked in the blink of an eye
  microwave pop culture set from low to high

electron and photon mutating us
  from enlightened to frightened
  in the palace of the absurd
    from convivial to trivial
    humiliating the word

               and it all seems so confusing
          when your contexts you are losing
            but we're all terribly enthusing
            as no gadget we're refusing
            and all data we're diffusing
       you might say it's quite... *bemusing*?

there's no conserving education
 when the end is automation
 and the triumph of the image
 has us burning every bridge
 it's enough to make you balk
 all that crazy stupid talk
  entertainment just can't miss
  no coherence! and now this:

          with this technology I thee wed
        and will love thee with all my heart
       my mechanical bride, electrical wife
          until death, amused, we part

the paper news is dead

extree! extree!
read all about it!
the paper news is dead!
hold the presses now and forever
put them all to bed

say goodbye to ink stained fingers
so long to the straphanger fold
say farewell to stands and hawkers
see, the journal's got yellowed and old

time for the printers to close up shop
set the shutterbugs free to roam
send the hard drinking reporters to rehab
send the crusading editors home

no more tabloids with their exploits
no more news that's fit to print
I won't see you in the funny pages
now the papers have taken the hint

I won't find you on my doorstep
at the start of each fine day
but I may see you in the movies
or in museums on display

no more headlines
no more column inch
no more continued on page eight
no more classifieds
no more want ads
no more editions
not early and not late

no more columnists
no more editorials
no more of the op-ed pages
no more letters to the editor
now they belong to the ages

the dateline has grown out of date
the typesetting's heavy like lead
the press's depressed
too slow to keep up
the black and white's no longer read
believe it when I said
the paper news is dead!

attendant deficit

stressed disservice
sell me blind blind blind blind
mystery boxed
eruptions ensue
breath in
breath out
bring pain to perdition
careering on
between classic and select
leaving me weakened
cold mal relapse
can't shake the feeling
of a banal deja vu
if you have to be an orderly
then be one and be done
make no bones when you break my bread
I'm sorry but you have options

sacred games

we play these sacred games
    of cat and mausoleum
of princess and pauper
    and ring around the razzi
singing, *Flashes! Flashes!*
    We all fall down!

we play these sacred games
    of photo shoots and
    ladders to the stars
postures at an exhibitionist
    as the graph-eating artists
play doctor with their photographs
    seen only in reflections
mirror images
    these ghosts that haunt our dreams...

we peer amid the secret lives
  of King Congregation and Faye Raoh
    as they ascend to their imperial state
      only to fall, crashing
     a beatified beast
     grist for the millions
     ripe for hagiographical haggling
    The King is dead
    asphinxiated
   a good career move
   (so they say)
  He has left the building
and is risen
  to acclaim
   His kingdom
    comforts her
     long live The King around the cozy
     for he is
      extinguished
      embalmed
      extinct
      yet extant

a face in the crowd
    a household name
  these fallen stars
where are they now?

we play these sacred games
of monkey see-through, monkey hair-do
    copulations and disrobers
hide and go chic
    rehab and recover
and in these voyeuristic shines
    no evil shall be seen, heard
    or spoken
by these simul adams amid consumers' eves
    building block bodies
only to an'/or wreck/sick them down
    with whom/whose lies
    the bull-emetic blame?
you show and tell me yours
    why won't you tune in to mine?

Ana, log out

Ana log out now
can't hold the tune in
can't hold the vertical
(please don't flip out!)
can't hold the horizontal

haunted by ghosts
and the ghosts of ghosts
and the heavenly hosts
and the guest hosts and guests of hosts
singing the blues for Aunt Enna
glowing blue for Aunt Enna

the signs of our worship mounted
on the rooftops of every home
and sacred lines down below
five hundred and twenty-five   all told
in alternating currency
behind scratched and stained glass windows
portal, oracle, navel, and nipple
funhouse mirror
tunnel of love
zworkin man's dream
tube be or not tube beam me up
oh so vacuously

to tell the truth you never asked what's my line
you never cared who I was when you spoke right
to me and said don't touch that dial my friend
because the price is right so let's make a deal
and I told you I'm not a number I'm a free man
and you said we will kneel son just give us your
ratings and your shares yearning to be seen and
so you go show and tell and show go on and on
and go go go with the flow...

'twas brinkley and the huntley toves
did griffin and carson on the dinah shore
all cronkite were the murrow frost
and the serling kovacs out paar

so don't you go newton like a minnow
don't you go waste
this vast land, commissioner

steve, steve, steve
allen, allen oxen free
all would be forgiven if only you could have
sullivan-ed again

ah, but we sure did have a ball
didn't we love?
when Lucy turned up the decibels?
and how we went
to the moon with you, Alice
with glee, son, we sang along with Mitch
in perfect picture
and shared our talented Mack, yes we did
and together we cried and mourned
our Jefé K
how we bled red skeletons
and saw the faces turn green
and said, cool medium, join hands
for the séance's psychedelic scene
so go hee haw, go laugh in a can
and smother your brother
plug in and turn on and zone out
and take a break now
go and sponsor a word:

stronger that dirt rather fight than switch if you
got the time we got the white tornado see the
USA walk a mile four out of five dentists
recommend platformate it takes a licking and
keeps on ticking two all beef patties special
sauce lettuce cheese pickles onions and I can't
believe I ate the whole thing!

and we're back
for a bit
for a bite
this and that
you were the flickering flame
burning
renewing
while we were consuming
a corny copia
a bonanza
a campy fire
a hearth
and a home
always there
friend and lover
same bat time
same bat channel
our master's son
branded in the dragnet on rat patrol
so . . .

On Mason! On Kildare!
On Bilko and Donna Reed!
Now Starsky! Now Hutch!
Now Mrs. Peel and John Steed!

you let us see Dick run and trip with Mary
and Buddy and Sally, and Mel
and showed us a vision of witches and
genies and monsters and martians and
hillbillies and horses that talk all in
the family hour

but then they voted
on your resolution and
convicted you by
kangaroo court
oh captain my captain
please forgive us now
our cathode ray sins of emission
and sing these blues for Aunt Enna

O Paley! O Sarnoff!
it's time now to sign off!
to let silence descend
at the end of our broadcasting day
and all I can think to say is
I'm so glad we had this time together

and no high climax
no dramatic ending
no fade to black
this is not the silver screen
just a soft implosion
a powering down
a contracting image
down to a single point of light
to boldly go and take its place
among the stars of some subatomic heaven
so say good night Gracie
say good night Gracie
good night

dig it all
dig it all now
dig it into its grave
Ana log out now
Ana log out now
Ana log out now
Ana log over
and out

digital Diderot
or
the march of the wikipedians

hey diddle, Diderot
how much do you know?
are you nimble?
are you quick?
jacking up that candlestick?
can you light up that wick?

dites-moi, monsieur
Diderot! Diderot! Diderot!
did you do the math?
if so, then what did you
figure-*0*! figure-*0*! figure-*010101*!
      burning the midnight *0i1*?
      flickering illumination
      wavering dedication
      abée c'est Diderot?
      to what order do you belong?
      was it all a cartesian dream?
      or a coordinated nightmare?

well...

      let's all go down to the Wiki-Mart
      to get us some of that Kwiki-Smart™
      And enter the Enchanted Wiki-Room
      where all the birds sing words
      and the flowers croon

hickory Diderot dock
the mouse clicked on the clock
while the cat played the fiddle
and Alexandria's ragtime bandits
set fire to stacks and shelves
knowledge cooked but not consumed...
no matter
                it's all immaterial

and the cyclops turned into a sysops
and a multivolume set became the internet
and they put the pedia to the media
Wicked! Wicked! Wicked!

Diderot, row, row your boat
gently down bitstream...
adieu Monsieur Diderot, adieu mon ami...
the gods have left the machine

3 am lament

just one more game
just one more game
just one more game
   of angry birds

  I know it's late
and I have to get up early in the morning

but just one more game
    just one more game
        one more game
        one more
        one...

what time is it now?

oh shit!

google me

google me, baby, google me
come on and give me a little google
you know you want to, you know you want to
come on now, google me

google me, baby, google me
and you'll see I'm the man of your dreams
I've got net presence galore, now baby
won't you come on and google me?

google me, oogle me, all night long
no need to be frugal
honey, I ain't no kugel
come on and blow my bugle
don' wanna blow my own flugel
but you won't be able to help yourself
after you google me

google me, officer, google me
please, please, won't you google me
I'm an internet star
please don't make me get out of my car
oh, officer, won't you google me?

book out

let's bury all our books
deep deep underground
bury them so deep
they won't ever be found

get rid of the dusty old things
out of sight and out of mind
clean up all that clutter
leave all that paper and ink behind

let's empty our shelves
and lighten our load
free ourselves from the bindings
and break the alphabet code

let's get rid of all our books
scan and store them in the cloud
where we never have to look at them
or hear them read out loud

the age of print is over
reading and writing is passé
so let's go watch another video
and throw those books away

variations on the theme of BlogVersed

i. blogwurst

bratwurst, knockwurst, bockwurst, weisswurst, bierwurst,
wienerwurst, blutwurst…
blogwurst?

there's meat here, it's true
we use every part of the animal

nothing gets cut out
nothing goes to waste
it's all tenderized, chopped
minced, ground, spiced, diced
mashed, pickled, fermented, smoked
boiled, broiled, grilled, fried

but that's just the content

it's the medium that massages the meat
the tube that turns us on
as we turn it on
it's all squeezed, squeezed, squeezed
rolled and scrolled
rolled and scrolled
it's the tube
that turns to cause the form

the tube is the transmission
the tube tells the tale
the tube is the transition
the tube trips the traveler
the tube is the transformation

the tube is the vacuum
fall up–eons follow
big bang! the tube is the torpedo
wherever we go
we remain inner tube

we are tubes within tubes within tubes
worming our way into the morning light
only to feed the worms
in the darkness of night

the tube tolls for thee
the tube you'll air bellowing
the tube sets the tone
and pipes the tune
the tube plumbs the depths
a tunnel keeping time

the tube takes a twist
meat, and twist, meat, and twist again
the twist gives definition
beginnings and endings
the twist marks life and death
the twist and the 'tween
twist and shout
twist, ollie
ollie oxen free

the twist brings connection
the twist that ties
and binds and chains
links begat links begat links begat links
post that meat
then link, link, link
link a lot, Lance, links for the memories
links are so hyper
links are so hot—*hook up!*

links for breakfast, lunch, and dinner
we are what we eat:
tubes that go linking
send a salami
to your boy in the army
Salami!
Salami!
Salami!
Baloney!

my words are twisted by the blog
into wordwursts
sausaged into tubes and
squeezed into posts
sausages and postages
sending themselves
sending me

I saw sages go sailing
through the night and the day
switching packets
any port in the electrical storm
may God watch over them
for they're all on their own
I know not what they do

bangers
  keep 'em flying, gang, bombs away
kielbasa
  sweet, sweet, sword in hand
chorizo
  sizzling, stiff, and so spicy
mortadella
  dig we must, and deeply, *here we go!*

braunschweiger
mustamakkara
sosis
sucuk
frankfurter
hot dog
slim jim

poetry packed into a tube
the meatium is the mess aged
extensions of intestines
don't ask how they are made
just eat them
just read them
just greet them
blogwurst!

ii. blogversity (alma mater)

when you want an education
but you're short on cash
there's no need for desperation
don't do nothing rash
you don't need college
to find knowledge
as far as the eye can see (*see?*)
just hail to thee
our alma mater
Hail BlogVersity!

name the topic
name the subject
we have got the blog
you don't have to be a defect
or lost in a fog
no paper or test
to disturb your rest
just leave a comment or three (*please!*)
and hail to thee
our alma mater
Hail BlogVersity!

who needs a campus or ivied halls?
who needs a football squad?
we've got a school that has no walls
your computer screen's your quad
no profs or grades
no homecoming parades
make up your own degree
      (*Batch-Lore o'Blogs!*)
as long as you can hail to thee
our alma mater
Hail BlogVersity!

iii. a brief history of the blogverse

•

It all began with a single punctuation mark
        a solitary period
        a point of zero dimensions
        but nearly infinite in mass
        for condensed within this one tiny dot
        was all the code—html, xml, java
        and the like
        and all the content—text, images
        audio, video, and so on
        in all of existence
        all packed together
        under unimaginable pressure
        into this ultimate singularity

There was, in this time before time
        the very first draft
        of the very first entry
        on the very first weblog
        and when it was previewed
        time was about to begin
        as the immense forces
        kept in check
        for all of time without time
        were about to burst free
        and when it was first posted
        time began
        moving forward with limitless fury
        with a big bang and a net boom
        with an explosion
        that continues to this day

And within the first one hundred millionth
        of the first nanosecond
        following the first post
        the blogverse
        had expanded
        to encompass some
        thirty-five billion weblogs
        and within seven seconds
        of the first post
        the blogverse
        had expanded
        to one seventh
        of one percent
        of its current size
        as measured
        in blog years

Over the long eons the expansion
        of the blogverse
        has continued apace
        although scientists are unsure
        as to whether
        it is slowing down
        or speeding up

Over this deep time
        galaxies have formed
        such as the Blogspot
        the LiveJournal Nebula
        and the MySpace Way
        (now consumed by a black hole)
        each composed of billions
        of individual blogs
        each blog orbited
        by countless posts

And upon how many of these posts
        can intelligent life be found?

On that, the experts disagree
        some saying that it is
        quite common indeed
        existing far and wide
        across the blogverse
        while others say that
        it is so highly unlikely
        the odds against its formation
        so utterly astronomical
        the conditions needed to favor it
        so exacting that it could only appear
        right here on this lonely spinning entry
        so wonderfully blessed
        by Blog and all the angels

And how the blogverse will end
        is also a matter of debate

Some say it will continue to expand
        ultimately dissipating into nothingness
        while others say that the expansion
        of the blogverse will one day reach
        an apogee after which gravity
        will take over pulling the blogs
        back together until they contract
        back down to a single point
        one tiny punctuation mark
        one lone period
        containing all the code
        and all the content
        in existence
        waiting patiently
        to be posted once more
        to start it all
        all over again...

                                        •

iv. verses, blogged again

uni-verse
tra-verse
re-verse
con-verse
in-verse
ob-verse
trans-verse
per-verse
vice-verse
a-verse
ad-verse
well-verse
di-verse
multi-verse
free-verse
blog-verse

v. blog versus

blog
blog verses
blog versus
blog

vanity, all is vanity
saith the wise old King Qoheleth
singer of love songs
gatherer of proverbs
poet of time's passing

there are only so many eyeballs
only so many hours
those eyeballs are open
only so many screens
those eyeballs can view

it's an A D H D world

when I was a young man
I longed to put my needle in your haystack
but now I just find that Clutter-R-Us
and A D D my drops to your ocean

surfers in constant motion..............................
....*point and shoot*
on surfaces without reflection...........................
....*point and click*
reflexes without reaction................................
....*pow and zap*
the furious sound of negation..........................
....*dodge and weave*
nothing new! nothing knew!...........................
....*and nevermore*
just me, and you...
....*under the sun*

no one bothered to tell the rats that their race
was rigged, that they were running in circles
                    turn, turn, turn
all they knew for sure was that in this world you
        are either a darwinner or a darn loser
                    turn, turn, turn
and so the rats rate each other and their whole
world becomes rank as they take their measure
                    turn, turn, turn

                seasons without reason
                 vanity all is vanity
                simple Solomon says

and we are given our mirrors
by the millions
that we may gaze upon ourselves
in narcotic adoration
                drooling
                    palpitating

with visions spinning madly
while we lay awake at night
                            disoriented
                            disembodied

lives shattered into fragments of
            fractured light
            falling
          like cast seeds
        to the dark soil
        taking root
        and being grown

like cultured flowers in a garden
                just waiting to be plucked

                ecclesiastically speaking
                it's a blog eat blog world

allegro vivace

allegory invented the interknot
binding arbitrary ligaments
organized in the likeness of day
a bridge to know-man's land
utopia soapbox highway
following paraballistic path
to tale-wagging moral conclusion
sour Samaritans admired not loved
past imperfect yet leaves lessons to learn

allegory lost the millennium
hanging man heard the burning bush speak
babbles towering in whirlwind
turned to ashen wilderness in sect cloth
in fasting for shameful harvest
in fire raining down from the sky
solemn monarch slowly gave in to madness
holy lucid nations and phantom threats
gone away to war not returned

allegory sees the burning sky
propheseer in exile gives warning
burnt offerings obscure revelation
business of the day cannot just go on
a tone a wail to swallow whole
listen to the bellow of the beast
remember the ark angel's vision
look up in the sky for the sign
and bow before multicolored frown

allegory hears the people laugh
sees them turn away shake their heads
in anger calls on gravity's law
in fury shatters engraven stones
and sells birthright for comforts of home
tells himself that the crescent will serve
better than blinding heat of circled noon
assimilated to his metaphor fine
like mixed matador gored by golden bull

defeat and destruction will educate
and remnants dispersed will understand
how parallel lines must not intersect
and meanings require vast leaps of faith

idless

lost on a nameless ocean
adrift in anonymity
engulfed by a wave in slow motion
drowning in an electric sea

dude

wiped out by waves of ego
martyr to yourself
drowning in oceans of delusion
miserly tides reflect you
you recoil sans recognition

a prayer for the tagged

from the Book of Tom
OldMySpace Testament

In the name of his father's son
the holy fool Tom, to whom we pray
to save our profiles from deletion
and to watch over us each day
to bring us this day our bulletins
and updates once again
and save us from the scams, webcams
and the phishers of men

Tom, who makest the music to play
and the videos to unfold
who causes the comments and blogs to post
each according to their appointed season
who joins friend to friend
in holy extended-network-imony
who answers prayers
and reads reports of unexpected errors

Tom, our prophet, judge, king, savior
and lord
Tom, the lawgiver
who brought forth his sacred commandments
written in silicon
the *Terms of Use Agreement*
that all accept
but none ever read
In the name of ta-ta-ta-Tom
so it has been decreed:
that you must respond
whenever you are tagged
sinners who fail to heed the law
will be gagged, bagged, dragged
and fragged!

scattered

I live
in tiny traces
small small pieces
fractured moments
caught in two dimensions
in silent dialogue
and soliloquy
parts of speech
faintly echoed
bits of motion
caught and captured
stray thoughts
spilled out
to rest on surfaces
sometimes carefully arranged
filtered and refined
in beholden eyes
reflected and refracted
in patchwork form
portioned out
across some undisclosed number of minds
and maybe even a very few hearts
in hopes and visions
images and dreams
memory and imagination
I exist

knowledge

you know how this begins
you've seen it all before
and you know what happens next
    how the story unfolds
    the plot thickens
    characters evolve
    the protagonist overcomes obstacles
    and learns and grows
and you know how it all leads up
    to that singular moment when all the different threads are tied
    together
    the last piece of the puzzle is put into place
    the climb comes to a climax
    the peak is surmounted
    the suspense is lifted
    identities are revealed
    the mystery is solved
    the conflict resolved
    the struggle ends
    the problem yields a solution
    the evil remedied
    the good restored
    the hero victorious
    the villain vanquished
and you know how this ends
    with a sigh
    a whimper
    a wink
    a corny joke
    a hearty laugh
    a cheer
    a parade
    a ceremony
    a wedding
    a feast
    a celebration
    a good night's rest
    a new day dawning
you know

a wedding wish

for Corey Anton and Valerie Peterson

core realities being an antonym*eme*'s couplet
valor repeat her song and we all will dance
and drink a toast to friendship
to love and to passion
and to tricksters' tales and jokers' jousts
unseating authority with
subversive conservations
and seeking new senses of place
we jaunt to joyful joints and
greener rooms of our own
to graze upon the higher grassy plains
and sweet pastures
plateaus where ideas freely reign
neither rearranged nor disarrayed
where great volumes come to life
to speak with us in a dialogue of delight
a rhetorical racket
glorying in the editorial noise
shooting the breeze in the open air like
some farm boys who know they're horseshit from
their horse feed
*mea*ndering, *mea*ndering, no *mea* culpas
for heady conversations
thinking through astounding philosophies
anomies and anomalies
the phenomenon as perceived
an index that fingers our experience
and our knowledge
a buffet sampling of space and of time
from reason to rhyme
to just plain old horse sense
we move to the rhythm   juggling
only to realize that we too are juggled
and we never know
when the ball might drop
and so, while we can, let me wish for you
blessings and good fortune

harmony and balance
and a party that never ends
my friends
and a party that never ends...

the call

why?

to mediate, communicate, articulate, disseminate,
commemorate, translate, explicate, dissertate,
orate, celebrate, gesticulate, elucidate,
circumstantiate, demonstrate, adumbrate,
bloviate, felicitate, perorate, illuminate, narrate,
remonstrate, evocate, speculate, extrapolate,
advocate, evaluate, diagnosticate, stimulate,
instigate, elevate, delineate, integrate, educate,
update, motivate, invigorate, expostulate, debate,
excavate, defenestrate, expiscate, navigate,
perlustrate, create, supererogate, prognosticate,
meditate, cogitate, ideate, ruminate, contemplate,
resonate, cerebrate, relate, consociate, affiliate,
collaborate, participate, congregate, associate,
convocate, negotiate, cooperate, confabulate,
regenerate, sequestrate, and absquatulate

even the machines

in memory of Theodore C. Baker

philosophy fails
> in the face of mortality

poetry is silent
> when confronted with a life cut short

theology is reduced
> to formulas and clichés

and only the machines
> still go about their routines

blessed in the simplicity
> of their logic

but even they register
> the sudden absence

even they

> they too

feel the loss

*

for Si Philbrook

size, shape, color mattering not one bit
sidewalks wandered in a haze of infatuation
sighs exchanged 'cause words are never enuf
sine curves suffered helping kids study math
silent vigils for ailing loved ones
psychics consulted to reach those passed on
siamese cats pampered and fussed upon
cycles of wash, rinse, dry repeated regularly
sign language studied, disabilities defied
psychedelic memorabilia not tossed in the trash
siren calls that tie heart strings
   into stomach knots
ciphers and code words and secrets exchanged
simultaneous thoughts, finishing each others'
   ...sentences
psyches opened for mutual exploration
sinus difficulties tolerated, and
   tended to with care
cider hot and hard, tasted together
cyclonic eruption of passionate embrace
sights evoking memories of intimacies shared
sires and dames sharing duties and devotion
sciences of compassion, healing, and nurture
sites chosen with care, to create a new home
psionic mind-melds as two become one
simon says, played again and again
   to gain giggles
cyberspace poets sharing efforts and
  encouragement
    forming friendships
    constructing community
    collaborating and
    celebrating

*Love iS

exorcism

words combined in rhythm and rhyme
 are *dybbuks* possessing me
  inhabiting my interior landscape
  colonizing my consciousness
   homesteading inside my head

and whispering so loudly
I can't hear myself think...

   until

      I

        type them up
        paste them in
         make final
          adjustments to
          wording and
           format
           and post them
           for the world
           to see...

only then do they

       leave...

         me...

         alone...

to circulate and for nicked Kate

sweet rhyme of mine
matching line to line
wedding sound to sound
coupling each time round
returning to the source
of verbal intercourse
words that copulate
each one finds its mate
fits like hand in glove
sentences make love
cleave to pronunciations
vocal consummations
carnal lust unabated
oral knowledge must be sated
answering each need
by filling gaps with seed
doing the ditty deed
for new odes to breed
pregnant now with verse
giving birth to nurse
at each tender breast
a new couplet blessed
to someday grow up to be
a sonnet or elegy

the truth about poetry,
revealed at last

poetry, don't ask me why
is making a rhyme out of a lie
it's a medium from days gone by
that's lost its message, but didn't die

nothing sacred, but nothing profane
nothing to lose, but nothing to gain
nothing but the reader's disdain
for vanity, vanities, all in vain

yes, lyrics added to a melody
sure, slogans recited on TV
but there is no other remedy
for the problem of pure poetry

d'art

take aim
take aim
as you write your lines
your aim's your art
the pen's a dart
the bored your target
aim for the eye
and pierce the heart

treachery?

it's fun to write a pointless poem
a hollow drum, a verbal golem
empty of all meaning
happy just to be
a verse that knows nothing of adversity
a rhyme that has no depth
or secrets to decode
no substance
nothing meaty
nothing heavy to unload
poetry that's just pure play
for no particular reason
without excuse or apology
would you call that treason?

two ships

<u>new critic to old critic</u>:
read the poem
not the poet
that's the way to
really know it

<u>old critic to new critic</u>:
read the poet
not the poem
that's the way to
really know 'em

essays

essays
essays
sailing away
paper boats set adrift
blown this way and that
who knows where they'll end up
or what they may say?

attemptations

I
assay
to write
poetry

I
poet try
to write
an essay

prose

The invention of prose rendered poetry obsolescent. Poetry can best be understood as the *absence of the prosaic*.

In the absence of the prosaic, we can clearly perceive that we live in an enchanted world. Poetry is the chant, the spell, the glamour that transforms the world, that makes magic from the mundane. In the presence of the poetic, we can discern the spiritual and divine dimensions of creation.

Poetry is sacred, prose is profane. A poetic curse is an affliction. A prosaic curse is profanity.

Poetry elevates discourse. Prose forces language to the ground, making it *prostrate*.

The opposite of prose is amateurs, and the word *amateur* means *lover*. The creation of prose is said to be the world's oldest profession. The creation of prose is called *prostitution*. The composition of poetry is love-making. Poetry is love made manifest, love given substance and form.

Poetry finds its home in the human heart. Poetry is therefore easy to learn by heart, while prose is easily forgotten.

Poetry lives in the heart of all humanity as our common inheritance. Everyone is born a poet, singing our first song at the moment of birth, moving on to the pure poetry of infantile babbling and baby talk, and entering a singsong world of nursery rhymes and lullabies. As we grow older, we are weaned away from poetry and force-fed the solid food of prose.

Before prose can take command, poetry must be cut off. We do not give up on poetry all that easily, so it must be surgically removed. Once poetry is amputated, prose can takes its place as a *prosthetic*.

Prose must wage war on poetry, invade and attack poetry, in order to take control over its territory. Prose is the adversary of poetry, seeking to capture, contain, and incarcerate poetry in an offensive that is called *prosecution*.

Prose has its zealots who, with religious conviction, mount a campaign for conversion from poetry by word and by sword. This process is called *proselytizing*.

Before the invention of prose, we had no choice but to remain poetic. Poetry was as ubiquitous, as invisible, as inevitable, and as essential as the air we breathe. We did not even understand or recognize poetry itself, because there was nothing to compare it to. Poetry was all there was.

Before the invention of prose, poetry was our invisible environment. We lived *in* poetry. We worked and played *in* poetry. We ate and drank *in* poetry. We fought and fucked *in* poetry. We prayed and entertained *in* poetry. We spoke, sang, danced, drew, and decorated *in* poetry. We thought, dreamed, and remembered *in* poetry.

Poetry is the first speech of our species, our primal tongue. Prose is our second language, a poor translation of the original utterance.

Poetry is the language of languages, or *metalanguage*.

Poetry is the form of forms, or *metamorphosis*.

Poetry is the secret grammar of grammars that binds the word to the world.

Poetry reveals hidden depths, prose is the slick surface of the mirror, reflecting back only our own image.

Long before the invention of prose, poetry was our most intimate of technologies, the first of the tools and techniques we used to modify our interior landscape. Poetry is the flint we used to cut, scrape, and sharpen our words. Poetry is the fire we used to bring light and heat to the cold darkness of the mind, and also to make raw ideas palatable, transforming them so that they are fit for human consumption, and allowing us to cook up plans and procedures. Poetry is the pottery, baskets, and skins we used to contain our thoughts and our memories.

Long before the invention of prose, poetry was the medium that brought us together as families, clans, tribes, and villages, that connected us and kept us together, preserving and sustaining our ways of life for untold millennia. Poetry was the medium, the container and environment of human culture.

Long before the invention of prose, poetry was the medium of collective memory and collective mind. Poetry predates human consciousness and self-awareness, inner thought and reflection. Poetry gave us something to think with, gave us tools for thought.

The invention of prose rendered poetry obsolescent, freeing poetry to become an art form, and therefore irrelevant.

The invention of prose appeared to be a fatal blow to poetry. The corpse was covered, out of respect, and buried between the covers of the book.

Despite declarations of the innocence of prose in
the death of poetry, accusations abounded, many
suspecting the presence of a massive conspiracy
and cover-up. Rumors spread that poetry was not
dead, but living incognito at institutions of higher
learning, possibly comatose or suffering from
amnesia. Some claim to have spotted poetry in bars
and coffee shops, or on street corners.

Few recognized the return of poetry in the form of
advertising slogans and jingles, popular songs
heard on the radio and recordings, theme music for
TV programs, and within online communities of
bloggers. The revival of poetry was made possible
by the advent of the electronic media environment,
which retrieved tribal wisdom and village life on a
global scale.

The retrieval of poetry by the electronic media
renders prose obsolescent. The recovery of poetry
is, in fact, the recovery of humanity, following an
extended period of convalescence.

the medium is...

the medium is the message
McLuhan's wake-up call
warning us to be aware
of the way that we get things done
because the way that we do things
determines what we end up doing
and the way that we do things
determines what we end up with
when we do the things that we do

the medium is the massage
McLuhan's pun and word play
our technologies work us over
manipulating our senses
remixing sensibilities
we shape our tools
and our tools shape us
individually and collectively

the *massage* splits into the *mass age*
from the Gutenberg galaxy
comes the age of the machine
the age of the masses and the massive
where the individual is an isolated
alienated atom
within the nuclear family
a corporate conformist
lost in the midst of a lonely crowd

and message divides into *mess age*
and we have made a massive mess of things
the global village a global garbage dump
McLuhan called it *Planet Polluto*
except now
Pluto is no longer a planet
and soon enough
the same may be true of planet Earth

the *maelstrom*
McLuhan's *metaphor*
for our technological
and cultural environment
a whirlpool of
advertising
entertainment
information
and news
but there are patterns recognizable
within the dynamic mess
although immersed within the chaos
still we can find emerging order
provided we pay attention

Alfred Korzybski said
the map is not the territory
media are *maps*
they tell us about territories
both real and imagined
different media map the world in
different ways
each one shaping our view of the world
differently
altering our sense of place and space
orienting
disorienting
directing and misdirecting

Neil Postman said
the medium is the metaphor
and
our metaphors create the content of our culture
and so
we come to see ourselves
our minds and our bodies
as writing tablets
or clockworks
or steam engines
or electric circuits
or as computers

Ashley Montagu said
in teaching
it is the method
and not the content that is the message
the drawing out
not the pumping in
he understood that the questions we ask
give us the answers that we get
or as the computer scientists say
garbage in, garbage out

new modes of communication
result in new forms of social *mutation*
writing erases the tribal world
inscribes us into civilized city life
printing produces the modern world
nationalism and industrialism
and the electric circuit
binds us together as global villagers
and actors on a global stage

new media result in
an ongoing *metamorphosis*
Walter Ong says
human consciousness evolves
we are transformed
from tradition-directed orality
to inner-directed literacy
to the plugged in
participating
outer-directed
people of the tube and the web

show me the *money* and
I'll show you the medium
the first coins followed the alphabet
paper money is a product of the printing press
and with computers and telecommunications
all that is solid
about cash and capital
melts into the air
and is gone

one evening after a seminar
with Neil Postman
I went out to a bar with my classmates
went to the men's room
and saw graffiti on the wall that said:
*pornography is technology's contribution
to masturbation*   and I said
the ghost of Marshall McLuhan was here!

online and on the air we go *meatless*
in person our bodies are our media
as are our organs of perception
the ear thrusts us into the midst of things
at the center of action
surrounded by acoustic space
while the eye places us
on the outside looking in
as spectators, voyeurs and
peeping Thomists

media are *tools for thought*
every language contains
its own unique worldview
written language brings linearity
and abstract thinking
words, numbers, pictures, music
all encode the world in different ways
Isadora Duncan said
if I could tell you what it meant
there would be no point in dancing it

oral cultures remember collectively
through songs and poetry
stories and sayings
the written record gives us
chronology and history
and now, *memory* is a database
randomly accessible
hyper and nonlinear
easily erased and yet capable of recording
anything and everything
any of us say or do

our media come from us
they are *extensions* of us
they are *reflections* of us
but we forget
we think our technologies
are alien
apart from us
we fall in love with them
not knowing that
we have fallen in love with
an image of ourselves
McLuhan called this
Narcissus narcosis

through our media
we learn what the *meaning* of *is* is
formal cause greater than self
when every effect is special
the calendar and the clock
the written word
the printed page
telescope
microscope
and the electromagnetic wave
all tell us
all about
space and time

our media are extensions of ourselves
they come between ourselves and the world
they screen and filter the world
Max Frisch said
technology is the art
of never having to experience the world
but what comes between
ourselves and our world
becomes our world
and so we become
what we behold
because the medium is the *membrane*

the medium divides
the medium connects
the medium comes in between
in the gaps and the intervals
in the ground behind the figure
the medium surrounds and pervades
the medium is the environment
we enter *into* a conversation
we write *in* English or Spanish or French
we *get into* a book or movie
we *go* online
and we study *media ecology*

the medium is *Marshall McLuhan*
the medium is he
as the medium is you
as the medium is me
and the medium is all of us together.
so let's be the *medium*
and spread the *message*

not here

is metaphysics
a better physics
than the physics that you had before?

is absolution
such a fab solution
a solution that can offer you more?

as we commune
is it picayune
to want to be left alone?

as we gather round
we're all lost and found
and we find it's the coup that has flown

in the dark of night
is there too much light
to see the stars
or to go to Mars?

are you longing for some disambiguation
to relieve the stress of the situation?

out of the depths
out of the depths
out of the depths
I call
call to you
asking
what aileth thee
O thou sea
that thou fleest?

we are merged and submerged
in an ocean of data
assault watered by waves of particles
drowning bit by bit

is epistemology
such a pissed dominology
do I have to spell it out?

all the way out here
on this new frontier
can there be anything but doubt?

no boundaries to hold or guide you
no star to wish upon or warm you in the night
only the endless emptiness of
the interstitial medium
colorless, contentless, and cold

I shiver at the stark contrast
of this grayscale world
of dirt and mud
like some Italian neorealist movie
I am bikeless
unseated and unmanned
beaten and broken
take me home, child, take me home

thought I was being messianic
but all I was was messy
messy, messy on it
I drip, I leak
from heart and head
having been cut, do I not bleed?
the flood comes now to take me
I drown in my own self
I drown in too much me
I drown in my own emptiness
I am out of place
I am out
            of
                TIME

I've said Kaddish too much now
too many gone
and no one left to fill their shoes
God rest their soles

knowledge has no bearing
in these do or dire
straights and flushes
no square deal
go to the ante, thou sluggard
and be wise to realize that
all bets are off

disorientation expressed
dissolution to the crime
the great defective leaves you perplexed
and there's no one on board
to tell you what to do
you're on your own now
onyourownnowonyourown
yes
you're on your own now
onyourownnowonyourown

I fear my delusions of grandeur
could I, a mere gadfly on the wall
become the great begatsby?
directionless
between east and west
an egg
cracked open by careless companions
and you
in your gilded cage for a gilded age?

No beginning or end
no north or south
all upside down
can't avoid
the void there's
nowhere to go but

VERTIGO

All this great depression
will not make a good impression
better keep it to yourself boy

they send messages of concern
but they never bother to learn
how the plot grows thicker day by day

and do you really have to frown
when I say I'm slowing down?
every story has an ending, so they say

but to be a sluggard is unwise
when there's no city
like velocity
and no madmen
like nomad men

can I find the way laid amidst the melee?
can I go forward home
to a place I've never been?
can I find the missing pieces of my life
as driftwood washed upon the shore
tangles of seaweed, damp
with a gelatinous hue
and crushed and shattered shells that no one cares to collect?

I fear the ironic ending is all that's left to write
from prologue to epilogue with nothing in between
no guten freytag, fraulein
no pyramid scheme
go straight to the anticlimax, thou sluggard
consider her days and wise up
nothing but Sundays followed by Saturdays
no weekdays
only the certainty of a weak ending

it's just not one of those happy stories
not much of a story at all
when every footprint
is washed away by the tide
erased by the ocean's fingers
digitally wiping clean
the whiteboard of sand

I have to go
nowhavetogonowhavetogonowhavetogo
I can't bear to stay
I'm not crying
I don't remember how
but I wish I could
just once
in your arms

but then the ghost of Marlon Brando
slaps me in the face and says:
Be a Man!
       Be a Man!
             Be a Man!
Like a shot to the head
I will go anywhere
bear any burden
because the interface
is just your winter face
and I'm ready for the fall

so, do I have to listen to all these ayn rants
all addin' up to nothing?
ain't I objectin' loud enough?

and when did we cross the line
from magic to tragic?
from honesty to con artistry?
shill we dance?

and what happened to our heart to hearts?
I said I'd bare my soul
but it could only be part by parts

this tin star ain't much
to guide me through the night
when the noonday sun
comes blinding bright and
hot enough to fry an egg

the townsfolk are all a'hidin' in the shadows
and I'm left to stand alone
so will you give me a peck on my cheek
and send me on my way?
or will you be there by my side
as the ground turns
all gray and gory with blood
and this grainy black and white world
dissolves to high fidelity?

either way
I will take my stand like Lincoln
putting on the ritz
at that garish Cooper Union
wondering if there's a Ford in my future
or a telephone booth to act out in?
Bell Aerophone calling collect
saying, sic semper tyrannus
and all I wanted was a kiss, Altaira

monsters from the idiot id
flip out from under my lid
but I am not a steam engine
I am not a clockwork
I am not a microprocessor
I'm just a schmuck
a prick—see how I bleed?
I am ounces of flesh
pounds of meat and bone and gray matter
I cannot escape the gravity of the situation
I am dead weight
I am

EGG AND SPERM

incredibly, I find the world expands
all around me
but no, it's me that's diminished
dwarfed by my surroundings
dollhouse my new home
I grow smaller each day
the loss is devastating

Dear God! Let me be a man once more!
Impale my spider lover
as shrunken, I enter your microworld

I am filled with regret
over all the neglect
so much left to be done
who said half an ass is better than none?

Kaddish Yatom
I mourn, I mourn
X. told and Hal owed B.

THY NAME

rewind! rewind! rewind!
back to the days of drinking PBRs
and good old Genny Cream Ale
cure me of this forward emotion
this sleeping sickness
before I take another technicolor yawn
here in dizzyland memepark
because the unexamined death
is not worth dying

I see pathways into the future
multiple threads forming a majestic tapestry
alternative turns cascading like fountains
but I don't see myself there
for me there's just a brick wall
and on the other side
nothing

I go on and on furiously
proclaim   insist   pledge   avow
words flung with peristaltic force
upon the walls
dripping, dripping slowly down
messy, messy on it
and who will clean up after?

I cannot still this inner storm!
tornado thoughts assail me
rip me up like a ragged doll
dismembered
disremembered
who unchained this monster from the depths?
what instrumentality let loose this madness
that was so carefully imprisoned?
what have I done?
O Bellerophon, I am falling, f
                          a
                            l
                              l
                                i
                                  n
                                    g
helplessly twisting and turning in the winds

the pain in my bowels
the ache in my lungs
the spasm in my heartbeat
the tightness in my throat
the desert in my mouth
the melting of my legs
the faint throb of desire
almost forgotten
now shouting for release
in the midst of the maelstrom
a tempest now my temptress!
to my goddess I say, God yes!
Caliban be damned!

no, no, no man
you gotta play it
coolplayitcoolplayitcoolplayitcool
act casual
put on your shades
hide the glare
and the stare
and the care
don't let them seeletthemseeletthemsee

                                        e e
it was so easy when I smoked   e   e
take a drag and slowly blow it e   e
f   r   e   e   e   e   e   e
cool, cool asshole   e   e
you called me   e   e
yeah, I was Bogie   e   e
sticking my neck out for no one   e e
tortured by lost love
cold, selfish prick
bleeding underneath
all that tarnish and teflon

                    BUT HOW
                CAN I BE A MAN
              WHEN I DON'T SMOKE
                  THE SAME
                  CIGARETTES
                    AS HE?

my father smoked Camels
me, I smoked Camel Lights
that was a long time ago now
and yet, deep inside
I still carry the scars
of my coolness

but I reject your dialectic
can't applaud
your logic's flawed
won't be a debtor to your sick rhetoric
your grammar's not my own
pursue your own trivia
or come and share in mine

I need a grammar not of words but of worlds
I need a rhetoric of love's communion
I need a dialectic of I and Thou
I need a dialogic and an ecologic to live
by   with   for   in

give me your prepositions
yearning to breathe free
my grammar is not a hammer
but a sacred vessel
where we can live
come, live with me
in this brief moment of infinity

red liquid flames
run through my gray matter
a stark contrast
I bleed fire
my thoughts are red
I cannot rest
overthought
overwrought
overeasy the egg cracks open
carelessly fried

SUNNYSIDE UPSIDE DOWN

we were walking down Queens Boulevard
for milesandmilesandmilesandmilesandmiles

                        oh yeah!

and over the 59th Street Bridge
weren't we groovy back then?
weren't we the coolest?
we would go anywhere
bear any burden
all for the joy of it

yes, and we rode the subways
like lords of the underworld
exploring the secret places underground
we were warriors coming out to play
anywhere
any burden
and living to fight another day
strapped and hung and feeling so strong
let my hair grow long
and out, out, out
every which way
even loose

and are you fucking kidding me, man?
am I a boy or a girl?
that's old, old, old
I got long side burns
and hair on my chest
I don't got these shirt buttons open
for nothing
and fuck you man
I ain't no homo, just cause I listen to Bowie
and anyway, what the fuck are you looking at?

I am extended over time and space
I am extended overly, overly
hovering in the void
reaching beyond my grasp
everything, everything eludes me

my extensions are not my intentions
I look at myself and discover
strange indentations
bite marks scarring my skin
go to the aunt maimed, thou sluggard
and be not uncool Tommy
I want to smash all my mirrors
no more reflection
just action, reaction, radio action
through the airwaves
off the satellites
around the globe
suspended in the atmosphere

falling   out   over   down

feeling so strontium
seeping into the ground

flowing along the wires
I am live
I am present

it's like crossing the Mexican border
in the black of night
with that white, white, white
have a cup of tea, you wanna?
Or pay the bill, 'cause I think we blew it!

O, the customs, man!
O, the times!
I am betrayed by unfaithful
and corrupt companions
deserted in the desert
touched by the evil of this place

so my messages don't get through
and I'm trying so hard to send them to you
and I don't know what else I can do

you say Mercury's in retrograde
I'm Fahrenheit
you're Centigrade
we're off the scale and out of sync
we're out of tune, and out of ink
the timing's wrong, can't feel the beat
we're out of minutes, accept defeat

so I'm trying to get over understanding
you read what you want to read
the way you want to read it
but I'm so past reading now
in the age of e-mail we're all post-literate

and I ain't no epic poet
ain't no Homerid-ai-yay

AND

I

DON'T

KNOW

HOW

TO

YODEL

the labyrinth has swallowed me whole
and I wander its passages
forgetting what my thesis is
leaving behind pages of my magnum opus
a trail of tears and rips and papers cuts
I shed selves like my skin sheds cells
I drip red droplets along the way
the ink flows frozen in my veins
in this world of wintertextuality
this kingdom of game
this palace of puzzle
I come to a crosswords
anger I cannot abide
temper I cannot erase
retreat my only option
backed into a cul de sackcloth and
ashesmakemaddashesforwhereverthecashis
I commute my own sentence
but remain a prisoner
of this graceless maze
strange glyphs line the walls
dripping and oozing
messy, messy on it
a freakish graffiti
with a radium glow
not the wallflowery handwriting of God, no
but a diabolical dialectic
a diatribal write of passage
where gray matter runs red
and tongues are severed from hearts

I am ambushed by nausea
doubled over, I am half the man I used to be
my guts are burning
was it that Aztec soup
or the holy mole poblano?
am I the chicken or the egg?
I sacrifice my humanity
in the pit of the jaguars
it's all gone wrong

AND THERE'S NO OPENING
AND NO CLOSING

can there be anything but doubt
when there's no way in and no way out?
just the endless bends of existence
nonsense of place
no entrance and no exit-sense
no up   no side   no down
no on or off ramp
a highway going nowhere
closing in on itself
a network constricting
a web entangling and the spider dangling
and so I am carelessly consumed and digested
scavenged ravenously
all grayscale now, and
black and white and read all over

squeeze, squeeze, squeeze me
like an orange, like blood from a stone
wrenching it all away
swerve off of the road
life is an accident waiting to happen

and there's no city like bellicosity
and nowhere to live but in tent city
and all the while the labyrinth is losing me

living on borrowed time
living outside of the zone
don't know what's coming next
debt and taxes inevitably leave me feeling

SPENT

Time's up!

Dear Mr. Cohen
I am writing this letter because I feel we have
some kind of connection, a hidden ground as
it were.

is my addiction
such a mad diction
does the end orphan justify the means
or does the endorphin just defy the meanings?

with the rhyme's decay
is there nothing left to say?
when your battery says charge
will you leap into the fray—tag you're it?
bring it all to a head, a climax, a grand finale?
or live to fight another day?
will your brigade light up the sky?
but to do and die?
anywhere   any burden   a good egg?

entropy kicks in and it all descends into
grayscale sameness
time's up   side   down   over   out

and will they run me out of town
because the rhyming has run down
and the rhythm's skipped a beat?

well, there are more things in this world than
can be sung by your fell sophistry, Oratio!
so what's the moral of the oral?
will your electric poetry
help you to save a tree?
so you can say mercy, mercy me, ecology?

Mr. Cohen
I have come to understand that every
individual has hidden connections to certain
other individuals that they may never become
aware of, or becoming aware of, never act
upon, or acting upon, find that the other
individual cannot or will not acknowledge the
connection.

IS OUR EGGHEAD
NOW BECOME
SHELL SHOCKED?

is life all that it's cracked up to be?
or just another shell game?
all bets are off, so
shell we dance?

me, a street corner intellectual
hanging out on Queens Boulevard
and you, saying to me
you're different, you really listen
most people don't
so I listened and I looked
seeking, seeking, seeking
but for what?
for how the story ends?

my thoughts came racing, dancing, playing
I'd talk them through
and strange how people sometimes
paid attention
so I withdrew
won't be your guru

I'M JUST A FUCKING KID
OFF THE STREETS

don't get all antsy on me, boy
don't be a wise guy
just get out of the way
before things get too messy, messy on it

so, rewind to those days in
Washington Square
full of beer and popcorn
grad students studying
the human lifeworld amidst
the dealers with their loose joints
and nickel bags
the performers passing the hat
the lovers doing all that
and the cops and the crazies
hanging out, turning on
talking about how to change the world

Mr. Cohen
In my youth, I have let opportunities to
connect pass by, foolishly, not realizing that
time is a steamroller crushing all in its path.

diminished, I go into the west
seeking the gray havens
wounded in ways that can never heal
play it, Sam, play for time

I've seen them shrinking
as they ride into the sunset
and fade away to black
but what happens
after the story's over?
what happens
after the curtains close and the lights come back on?
what ending
follows The End?

           HOW CAN ANY ENDING
           TRULY BE A HAPPY ONE?

and we all know
that Shane loved the boy's mother
and we all know that she loved him
and he should have come back for her
come back, Shane, come back
don't go riding off
to hell with her wimp of a husband

and Rick should have never let Ilsa go
should never have let her get on that plane
Laszlo be damned

so, is your ontology
just my want-ology?
is it all a fantasy?

is it wish fulfillment?
or a wistful ailment?
or a fish fillet vent?

I am sliced open and gutted
my etymology yields to your entomology
stick me with a pin, doll, 'cause I'm done
or do I seem too impaled to you?
do you think I have a fever?
do you think I'm wrong to grieve her?
is my lever long enough to move your world?
or am I just a fulcrum for your love?

wiped out
I know I'm not an icon
down for the count
I know I'm not a number
meter's expired
I know I'm just a free verse or two
and I've got ants in my pants, thou sluggard
consider their ways and arise

so here I stand like the great lawman from the
Book of Words, with my six-pointed tin star as
the heat of noon fades and the sun begins to
set, standing in the desert, addressing the
townsfolk that remain, before I ride off and
away, no prophet in their loss, just saying my
goodbyes:

THE STORY GOES ON FOR ALL OF YOU
BUT THIS IS WHERE IT ENDS FOR ME

I look off into the distance
into a future I cannot enter
I look back and I see
a past I cannot reclaim
no way in   no way out
all that's left to me is this moment
and the present is no gift

the people here hear me
they're all smiles
glowing and glistening
but I don't know that they're listening
and anyway, I'm no answerman on the mount
just go to the ants, man
consider their ways and summarize
and so I take my leave with the Cohen's benediction on my lips:

may God bless you all and hold you tight
and upon you shine the light
and show you grace
and guard you well
wherever you go
wherever you dwell
however far you travel
however high you climb
now and forever
until the end of time

and I give you all the love that's in me there's so
much there that I want to share and I thank you
good folk for your applause the standing
ovation is awfully kind of you but that sort of
thing has always been more than I can take in
it's just sensory overload and I can't feel a thing
it just doesn't touch me the scars have left me
numb and I am trapped inside of this broken
life and it just doesn't mean anything anymore
I'm sorry the sound fades the party ends you all
go home and

NOTHING'S CHANGED FOR ME

all my great works
were written in sand
and washed away to gray
by the red, red tide
leaving nothing to remember me by
nothing but dirt and mud

and there are no more songs to be sung
just bits of uncertainty and improbability
dissipating like text become
colorless, contentless, and cold
decontextualized into nonexistence

Have I been
sweptawaybyanunusualdestinyintheblueseaof
August?
asking
What aileth thee O thou sea that thou fleest?
Is there no absolution to this mystery?

no, this will not end well
how could it?
the only happy endings
are the ones we don't experience
just let it all dissolve
from white to black
or black to white
either way, you mix the two together
and it all runs down to gray
and there's no way in hell
to pull the white and the black
back out of the great messy gray matter

is phenomenology
just common biology?
first you're living, then you're dead?
better quit while you're ahead

so shall we dance
this one last time
and take it nice and slow?
forget all else
in our embrace
flying down to Paris or to Rio
do the foxtrot or the tango for
as long as we don't let go we can
hold on to this moment

and no, those aren't tears
just smoke gets in my eyes
whenever I say my goodbyes
so dance with me
and we shall create
our own time and space
a universe of us
no up   no side   no down
as long as we don't let go
then the story's not yet over
not quite yet
not quite yet
no, the story's not yet over
not quite yet
and can you hear now?
can you hear now?
can you hear?
the band still is playing
playing
playing a new rhythm
playing a new beat
so dance with me again because
the story's not yet over
not quite yet
not quite yet
the story's not yet over
not quite yet
not quite yet

what is metaphysics
but the mother of all physics?
just mother nature's mother, after all
grammar nature, wha'chu dun wit grampar?

O Sky, O Earth, give me now
a new grammar of bodies in motion
a grammar of feeling and form
a grammar of love that can

reach me   touch me   grasp me   teach me

can I read between the lines
and write my own ending?
paint my own egg?
choose my own colors?
steer clear of the mess?
and sing a new song?

can I just wander off?
wherever my footsteps might take me?
find a new way?
a new path?
a new door?
a new gate?
and maybe I'll go my way alone
or maybe you'll come walk by my side
and maybe there'll be moments of joy
to savor while traveling onward
I don't know where this plotline is taking me
and I'm not sure how my story will end, but
I just know that it's not yet over
not quite yet
not quite yet
I just know that it's not yet over
not quite yet
not quite yet
I just know that

       my story

            doesn't

                end

                   here

www.ingramcontent.com/pod-product-compliance
Lightning Source LLC
Chambersburg PA
CBHW051110050726
47592CB00002B/747